THE GADFLY AFFAIR

A 21st Century Heretic's Excommunication from America's Most Liberal Religion

Todd F. Eklof

The Gadfly Affair

A 21st Century Heretic's Excommunication from America's Most Liberal Religion

Todd F. Eklof

Oakleaf Press
P.O. Box 19542
Spokane, WA, 99224

Copyright © 2021 by Todd F. Eklof
All Rights Reserved
ISBN: 9798719017433

For

Rev. Richard Davis, who bravely served as my Good Officer during a tumultuous time, suffering repercussions to his own career and ministry because of it. I could not have borne the aftermath of *The Gadfly Papers* without his friendship, support, encouragement, and courage. If history remembers me as Unitarian Universalism's pesky gadfly, this brave and gentle soul should be remembered as its mightiest defender. "Nothing in the world is as soft and yielding as water. Yet for dissolving the hard and inflexible, nothing can surpass it."

And For

Terry Steichen, another defender of the Unitarian Universalist faith and its historic commitment to free thought, free expression, and religious toleration. Although he worked behind the scenes, his wisdom, guidance, and analytical skills were crucial in the formation of our responses to the Unitarian Universalist Ministers Association and the Ministerial Fellowship Committee during the difficult year following the release of *The Gadfly Papers*. His name does not appear in any of the documents he helped draft, but he was crucial in the effort and has my deepest gratitude.

And For

The Members and Friends of the Unitarian Universalist Church of Spokane for their support and for enduring so much of the unnecessary conflict that occurred in the aftermath of the publication of *The Gadfly Papers*. It has been my life's greatest privilege to serve as your minister and your friend. Despite the difficulties we have endured together, I am confident history will look back, as will the future members of our historic congregation, and conclude ours was among its finest hours.

CONTENTS

PROLOGUE i
INTRODUCTION iv
SWATTED 1
BANISHED 8
CONDEMNED 16
PILLORIED 25
FLOGGED 41
EXCOMMUNICATED 56
ENDARKENED 76
AFTER WORDS 95
APPENDIX A 99
APPENDIX B 129
APPENDIX C 139
APPENDIX D 174
BIBLIOGRAPHY 185
INDEX 188

PROLOGUE

I must needs answer you freely that I esteem that toleration to be the chief characteristic mark of the true church.
—John Locke

IN HIS BRIEF HISTORY of Unitarianism, *For Faith and Freedom*, Rev. Charles Howe reminds us that it emerged from a separate though corresponding reformation with the Protestant Reformation of the 16th century. "Unlike Martin Luther," he says, "who retained many of the organizational and liturgical practices of Catholicism," and John Calvin, who "attempted to place, not only his system of doctrine, but also his system of church organization and worship, on a firm biblical basis . . . There were those—and their numbers were large—who were seeking a religious community of free spirits, one with no set standards of belief, little formal organization, and no prescribed forms of worship; instead they were seeking firsthand religious experience through direct communion with God."[1]

This new and liberal approach to theology, which gave deference to the individual over priests and preachers, and to humanity over church dogma and hierarchy, initially resulted in the Anabaptists, a group of believers who so greatly valued individual freedom that they rejected the validity of infant baptism, believing one's religion should be freely chosen by willing and thinking adults. They were the first to begin baptizing adults who had already been baptized as infants. Hence, their name, which means "re-baptizers." They also wanted a religion, as Howe says, "completely free of state control,"[2] which wasn't well received by the leading figures of the Protestant Reformation. This eventually led to the issuance of a formal death decree in 1529. They did their best to push back but, "Following a bloody uprising by the Anabaptists in the city of Munster in 1535, thousands throughout the region were put to death, either by drowning, beheading, or burning. The leaders of the uprising were horribly tortured and executed, and their bodies were suspended in cages from a church tower, where they remained until 1811!"[3] Can you imagine going to a church where the bodies of heretics remained on display for 276 years? Authoritarians intimidate their subjects by making chilling public examples of any who defy them.

PROLOGUE

The Anabaptists may have been persecuted out of existence, but their remnants went on to become those groups we know today as Baptists, Mennonites, and Unitarians, all of whom continue to maintain an independent church structure and congregational polity. Each has also struggled at times with internal authoritarian forces working to undermine such independence and freedom. Only 32 years after the massacre, Unitarianism was formally born in Transylvania when King John Sigismund Zápolya chose it as his religion during the 1567 Diet of Torda. A year later, he passed the Edict of Torda, a law protecting freedom of conscience and religious tolerance by guaranteeing "no one shall be reviled for his religion by anyone . . . and it is not permitted that anyone should threaten anyone else by imprisonment or by removal from his post for his teaching."

Although American Unitarianism emerged somewhat independently from its older, Eastern European cousin, it has been historically no less committed to the principles of religious freedom and tolerance. Like the founders and framers of the United States, America's brand of Unitarianism was inspired by the Enlightenment philosophy, summarized by Immanuel Kant as "the courage to use one's own understanding." The renowned Unitarian Rev. A. Powell Davies, minister of All Soul's Church in Washington, D.C. from 1933 until his death in 1957, called democracy our nation's true spirituality, even if it is often resisted by other religions that prefer authoritarian governance maintained by dogmatism. When speaking of the origins of American Unitarianism, in particular, he reminds us that President John Quincy Adams, Vice-President John C. Calhoun, journalist Joseph Gales, who was personally advised by Thomas Paine to start his revolutionary *Sheffield Register*, and other Enlightenment leaders were among the founding members of his congregation in 1821, and among the earliest of Unitarians. "So, by this time," he says, "were many, if not most of the leading figures throughout the country, including [Thomas] Jefferson."[4]

After the American Revolution, Powell says, it was only natural that they should want to "form a church which was definitely based on freedom. As over against the free thinkers outside the churches, they wished to be free thinkers inside the churches, lest too much that is essential to religion might be cast away."[5] If the Renaissance liberated humanity from the authoritarian Dark Ages, the flourishing of its principles during the Enlightenment, the Age of Reason, would help deliver America and its churches from the authoritarian colonialism and tyranny it had been founded upon. This is the reason Davies says, "Authoritarian systems, whether of church or state, are not American, and they cannot become American."[6] As a liberal religion founded upon this same principle, the same is true of Unitarianism: *Authoritarian systems are not Unitarian and cannot become Unitarian.* This is why, as the great 20th century Unitarian theologian James Luther Adams once said, "Free choice is a principle without which religion, or society, or politics, cannot be liberal."[7] Free choice is also a principle without which Unitarianism cannot be Unitarian.

---

[1] Howe, Charles A., *For Faith and Freedom*, Beacon Press, Boston, MA, 1997, p. 12f.
[2] Ibid., p. 13.
[3] Ibid., p. 13f.
[4] Davies, A. Powell, *America's Real Religion*, Beacon Press, Boston, MA, 1947, p. 27.
[5] Ibid.
[6] Ibid, p. 28.
[7] Adams, James Luther, *On Being Human Religiously*, Stackhouse, Max L., ed., Beacon Press, Boston, MA, 1976, p. 15.

INTRODUCTION

To find yourself, think for yourself.
—Socrates

My definition of a free society is a society where it is safe to be unpopular.
—Adlai Stevenson

The most courageous act is still to think for yourself. Aloud.
—Coco Chanel

ON AUGUST 16, 2019, I received a letter of censure from the Unitarian Universalist Ministers Association (UUMA) for having written and distributed my controversial book, *The Gadfly Papers*, during the Unitarian Universalist Association's (UUA) 2019 General Assembly in Spokane, Washington, just two months earlier. The UUMA made the letter public in a widely dispersed email announcement the following day. The next day, the local news media showed up during services at my church, but not to interview me about the censure as I first thought. I then guessed they wanted to discuss our controversial guest speaker that day, a man who was about to make history by becoming the first Jewish Rabbi to advocate for Palestinian rights during a Unitarian Universalist church service. Only a few months earlier, some in our local Jewish community began calling me anti-Semitic for planning to host a film on the topic.

But neither the letter calling the Spokane community's most liberal minister a white supremacist nor charges of anti-Semitism were reason enough for the news crew's visit that day. Unbeknownst to me, rather, the day after my own religious organization publicly condemned my use of logic as a tool of "white supremacy culture," the TV reporter informed me my name had appeared on a watch-list distributed to a white Christian identity militia by Washington's right-wing State Representative Matt Shea in a sixty-page manifesto reportedly calling for a holy war and the killing of resisters and liberal activists. It genuinely felt like I was in an episode of the *Twilight Zone*, having been accused of being a white supremacist on one day and learning I'd been targeted by a genuine white supremacist the next. As opposite as they may seem, however, Matt Shea and the UUMA do share something in common: an extreme unwillingness to tolerate viewpoints other than their own.

Much has happened since then, and since my distribution of *The Gadfly Papers* during the UUA General Assembly a short time earlier. During the following year, I was banned, condemned, fired, censured, and excommunicated from the fellowship of Unitarian Universalist ministers, and subsequently dismissed from membership in the UUMA. During the course of all this, much misinformation and many groundless rumors have also been spread on social media and by the UUA and UUMA. Rather than acknowledging the obvious, that both these entities have acted punitively to suppress a book critical of the direction in which they are leading Unitarian Universalism, they have shifted the blame onto its author by making up false claims that are easily disproven.

Although reluctant, I have been persuaded of my ethical obligation to explain all that has transpired during the year following my release of *The Gadfly Papers*. This isn't merely to set the record straight now, but for those historians tasked someday with looking back to explain what actually occurred. Hopefully, they will do so to learn about what *almost* happened to Unitarian Universalism, rather than what *did* happen to it. With this in mind, I have cited much of the documentation at my disposal, most of which has also been included in my appendices, although many individual names and other identifying points of information have been redacted.

The point of this book, like *The Gadfly Papers*, is to address the waning of the Enlightenment principles that American Unitarianism, in particular, is rooted in and, until recently, has been intertwined with. Like many Liberal organizations today, Unitarian Universalism is becoming overshadowed by an encroaching Age of Endarkenment, not unlike that which occurred during the Middle Ages. This is why my chapter titles reflect various Medieval punishments—*Banished, Condemned, Pilloried, Flogged, Excommunicated*—save for the last, entitled *Endarkened*, in which I focus on my larger concern regarding the dark age of suppression and retribution facing us all.

By now I have gotten used to being unjustly condemned for demonstrating my values in meaningful ways. In 2004 I was fired from my job after taking a public stand supporting gay marriage. In 2019, as noted, I was accused of being anti-Semitic for expressing public care and concern for Palestinian people, a clear effort to both discredit and silence me. Within hours of releasing *The Gadfly Papers* that same year, I was banned, condemned, and subjected to a barrage of words from the arsenal of character assassination—*racist, homophobic, transphobic, ableist, classist*—all for the purpose of discouraging anyone from actually reading what I had to say and, moreover, from daring to write anything like it.

These collective *ad hominem* responses to *The Gadfly Papers* immediately tried to make my book be about racism rather than what it is about: my concerns regarding the punitive, authoritarian, chilling, and otherwise illiberal turn Unitarian Universalism has taken. It would seem that kneejerk accusations of racism and the like against anyone unwilling to get with the program are the UUA's and UUMA's primary method of silencing dissenters these days, but there are many nonwhite luminaries in today's society expressing concerns similar to mine. John McWhorter, Coleman Hughes, and Irshad Manji are among those whose courage and brilliance most inspire me.

In his December 23, 2018, *Atlantic* article, "The Virtue Signalers Won't Change the World," John McWhorter, an accomplished linguistics professor at Columbia University, says antiracism has morphed "from a pragmatic mission to change minds into a witch hunt driven by the personal benefits of virtue signaling, obsessed with unconscious and subconscious bias. As noble as this culture of shaming genuinely seems to many, it's a dead end."[1] Likewise, in an August 19, 2020 article, "Toward a Better Anti-Racism," opinion columnist and writer Coleman Hughes calls this approach "a zero-sum power struggle between oppressed groups and oppressor groups—and . . . a win for the former requires a loss for the latter."[2] Unwilling to allow those he considers illiberal to own the term, Hughes advocates for a better kind of anti-racism:

> . . . that reaches back to Martin Luther King, A. Philip Randolph, Bayard Rustin, Frederick Douglass, and beyond. It is an anti-racism grounded in the idea that there is a single human race to which we all belong—and that all the ways of dividing us up, though they may be important to understand our present reality, should not be given moral weight. That is the principle that ultimately conquered slavery and Jim Crow—and it is the principle that ought to be revived today.[3]

This is not unlike the argument I make in *The Gadfly Papers*, which those who chose to criticize without reading it obviously missed: "This is not to suggest Unitarian Universalism should not continue concerning itself with those grave issues of injustice impacting specific groups, only that doing so requires a corresponding emphasis upon our common humanity":[4]

By retreating into Identitarian Segregationism, which may be a more apt name for what it has become, Unitarian Universalism also severs itself from the one shared taproot that brought us together to begin with, the recognition that all people share a common humanity and we must, therefore, continue working together as one united family, no matter our differences.[5]

Likewise, while guest speaking during an October 25, 2020 joint service for the Unitarian Universalist churches of Salem, Oregon and Spokane, Washington, bestselling author Irshad Manji called the Critical Race Theory that much of today's racial justice work is based on "dangerous." While acknowledging the good intentions of its advocates and some of its positive outcomes, Manji says, "The problem is that Critical Race Theory has ceased to be a philosophy and has instead become a dogma, an organized religion that verges on aspects of Fundamentalism." In her 2019 book, *Don't Label Me*, Manji further points out that "much of critical theory has itself become a drill in thoughtless conformity."[6] Although not on par with "Donald Trump's conspiracy peddling," Manji says, "I do, however, believe it's time to mature out of the bad habits that critical theory shares with delirious Trumptitude."[7]

Despite legitimate concerns expressed by good-hearted and intelligent individuals like these, the UUA and UUMA seem determined to ignore them, reverting instead to an underdeveloped way of thinking that is authoritarian, punitive, dualistic, absolute, and dependent. This is the opposite of the maturity of thought indicative of the Enlightenment thinking that Unitarian Universalism is founded upon. As philosopher Immanuel Kant wrote in his 1784 essay, *An Answer to the Question: What is Enlightenment?*, "Immaturity is the inability to use one's understanding without guidance from another."[8] Worse than merely demonstrating such primitive behavior, however, the leaders of our liberal religion are now demanding such stunted thinking from all of us by making examples of anyone who disagrees with their particular and, in the opinion of many, destructive approach to racial justice.

So, again, this book isn't about what has happened to me, but about what's happening to Unitarian Universalism, to liberalism in general, and to whole of Western culture, all of which are upon the frightening threshold of a new Age of Endarkenment. Those of us who care must counter with a new Renaissance, like that which helped humanity emerge from the original Dark Ages centuries ago. This is going to be a heavy lift given the groundless conspiracy theories, AI-driven echo chambers, and alternate facts influencing so many in today's societies. To accomplish this monumental task, we will need to become courageous advocates of those grand

INTRODUCTION

aspirations that have illuminated the dark nights of humanity's soul for the past 2,600 years—freedom, reason, tolerance, and our common humanity. Let us begin.

---

[1] McWhorter, John, "The Virtue Signalers Won't Change the World," *Atlantic*, December 23, 2019.
[2] Hughes, Coleman, "Toward a Better Anti-Racism," Manhattan Institute, www.manhattan-institute.org, August 19, 2020.
[3] Ibid.
[4] Eklof, Todd F., *The Gadfly Papers*, Oakleaf Press, 2019, p. 17.
[5] Ibid., p. 75.
[6] Manji, Irshad, *Don't Label Me*, St. Martin Press, New York, NY, 2019. p. 199.
[7] Ibid.
[8] Kant, Immanuel, *An Answer to the Question: What is Enlightenment?* Konigsberg, Prussia, September 30, 1784.

SWATTED

I am that gadfly which God has attached to the state, and all day long and in all places am always fastening upon you, arousing and persuading and reproaching you. You will not easily find another like me, and therefore I would advise you to spare me.
—Socrates

WHEN TITLING MY controversial book, *The Gadfly Papers: Three Inconvenient Essays by One Pesky Minister*, it was these words, which Plato attributed to Socrates, that I had in mind. He compared the State to "a great and noble steed who is slow in its motions owing to its very size, and requires to be stirred to life."[1] As a person of great virtue, devoted to doing and saying what he believed was right regardless of the personal consequences, including at the expense of his own life, Socrates considered it his duty to "stir" this once dignified creature back to life by becoming a pain in its butt. While I would ne'er compare mine to the wisdom or virtue of one so exceptional as Socrates, I too felt it was my duty as a modest, though devoted, Unitarian Universalist minister to help stir my once venerable liberal religion back to life with a few troubling essays.

The Gadfly Papers was written to remind Unitarian Universalists everywhere who we are and what we are about by recalling where we come from and showing how far we have strayed from those values that once held us steady. American Unitarianism, in particular, is rooted in the Renaissance principles that ended the millennium-long Dark Ages near the start of the 14th century, then flourished during the Era of Enlightenment beginning in the 17th century. For a thousand years prior to the Renaissance, every word uttered, written, or even thought in Europe, as well as all music, art, philosophy, and science, had to be spoken or otherwise expressed in orthodox Christian terms. Humanities professor A.C. Grayling says even "Moral discussion was restricted to interpretation of scripture and Church teaching, and any divergence from orthodox doctrine on these matters was for a long time heavily punished. But the beginning of modern times saw a return to the kind of debate about ethical principles that had flourished in Antiquity."[2]

The unparalleled Age of Antiquity began near Athens around 600 BCE, during which humankind took a giant mental leap forward, beginning with the first known Greek philosopher, Thales of Miletus. Thales is the first person known who sought to explain the nature of existence in natural, rather than supernatural and mythical, terms. Those philosophers who followed in his immediate footsteps, the *Presocratics* as they are now classified, attempted to do the same, resulting in the discoveries of atomic theory, musical octaves, irrational numbers, evolutionary theory, heliocentrism, scientific experimentation, medicine, and much more. Science began emerging simultaneously with Greek philosophy. This is why, rather than "philosophers," Aristotle referred to the Presocratics as *phusikoi* ("the physicists"). This unprecedented advance in human thought is also why Bertrand Russell says, "The rise of Greek civilization which produced this outburst of intellectual activity is one of the most spectacular events in history. Nothing like it has ever occurred before or since."[3]

Regrettably, this exceptional period of intellectual freedom and progress came to a crashing halt with the Christianization of the Roman Empire in the 4th century CE, after which Christian zealots are estimated to have destroyed "as much as ninety percent of the literature of antiquity."[4] This correlated with, if not caused, the emergence of the Dark Ages, which were marked by rigid orthodoxy lasting hundreds of years. Philosophers still philosophized during this period, but they too were mostly apologists for Christendom's *status quo*, gravitating more toward Aristotle and Neoplatonism than the ideas of the intellectually liberated *phusikoi*. Although some of them are considered to have made major contributions to Western philosophy, including Augustine and Aquinas at its bookends, most philosophers during the Dark Ages were also Catholic priests or monks who used philosophy to bolster Christian orthodoxy, especially in their attempts to prove the existence of God and explain or explain away the existence of evil. Conversely, those who allowed Antiquity's "pagan" influences to overshadow orthodoxy did not fare well.

Aristotle's logic, which allowed for inferences derived from ideas considered self-evident truths (*a priori*), helped to justify unsubstantiated beliefs in just about anything, and Neoplatonism addressed the existence of evil (also called the "Problem of God") by considering it merely the absence of good and, therefore, nothing that actually exists for which God, as both Creator and All in All, can be blamed or with which God can be associated. Neoplatonism also allowed for beliefs in nonmaterial entities including a deity. With these exceptions, Greek philosophy was treated with suspicion by the religious authorities for hundreds of years. In 529 CE, Emperor Justinian went so far as to abolish the nearly thousand-year-old Platonic

Academy because of its "pagan" teachings; "intellectual activity fell under the authority of the Church, and as time went by it became increasingly risky to diverge from doctrinal orthodoxy," Grayling reminds us. "Doing so could and too often did attract the severest of sanctions: the death penalty."[5]

Such stricture began to relax in the early 14th century, marking the start of the Renaissance, which is synonymous with terms like *rebirth, renewal,* and *recovery*, referring to the recovery of the discoveries of Antiquity. Although the Protestant Reformation was not the only contributor to this reawakening, it did weaken the Church's authority in certain parts of the European world, making it possible for some to begin thinking and speaking outside the confines of Christian orthodoxy. Some even began practicing what have come to be classified as Antiquity's occultisms, like astrology, alchemy, and magic. If the concept of *magic* hardly seems enlightened, it should be understood that at the time what seemed like "magic" was the result of experimental attempts to understand the workings of nature. As Bertrand Russell explains, "Magic is based on recognition of the principle of causality, that given the same antecedent conditions, the same results will follow. Magic is proto-science."[6] What seemed like magic at the time was based on an emerging understanding of physics, not in defiance of it.

Russell further points out, "Whereas the medieval scene was dominated by preoccupations concerning God, the Renaissance thinkers were more interested in man. From this circumstance the new cultural movement derives the name of Humanism, the second of the great new influences."[7] To the north this manifested as a more humanistic kind of Christianity that included respect for the theological autonomy of the individual through concepts like the "priesthood of the believer" (that there was no need of an intermediary between oneself and God). To the south, beginning with the Italian humanists and eventually spreading elsewhere, a more secular humanism emerged, accompanied by a unique tolerance and appreciation for all religions. Rather than fearing and forbidding those unorthodox views once dismissed as "pagan," a newfound appreciation developed for "all the literary classics of Antiquity—poetry, essays, letters, histories and biographies, philosophy,"[8] writes Richard Tarnas in *The Passion of the Western Mind*. "Ancient culture was a source not just for scientific knowledge and rules for logical discourse, but for the deepening of and enrichment of the human spirit."[9] Classical literature has since become known as the *Humanities*, which have remained the core of a modern Liberal Arts education (although they are currently afforded decreasing value in the widespread endarkening of academia).

In addition to valuing humanity's diversity of beliefs, Renaissance Humanism, freed from Christian dogma, especially that of Original Sin, gained a more elevated view of human nature. In his *Oration on the Dignity of Man*, the 17th century Italian humanist and devout Christian Giovanni Pico della Mirandola wrote, "Dumb creatures, as soon as they are born, bring with them, as Lucilius says, from their mother's womb all that they will ever possess. . . . But upon man, at the moment of his creation, God has bestowed seeds pregnant with all possibilities, the germs of every form of life. . . . if rational, he will reveal himself a heavenly being; if intellectual, he will be an angel and the son of God."[10]

Philosophers also began promoting the notion that societies and their governments ought to exist for the purpose of upholding the dignity of their citizens by assuring them the freedoms necessary to flourish as individuals. Baruch Spinoza, my fellow heretic, who was exiled from his synagogue in 1656 for "'abominable heresies" and unspecified "monstrous deeds",[11] and whose rational philosophy would have tremendous influence on the coming Enlightenment, once said, "Everyone is by absolute natural right the master of his own thoughts, and utter failure will attend any attempt in a commonwealth to force men to speak only as prescribed by the sovereign despite their different and opposing opinions."[12] This sentiment was greatly amplified during the next two centuries of Enlightenment, also known as the Age of Reason, when the admiration of classical thought seeded during the Renaissance began flourishing throughout Western culture.

In *An Answer to the Question: What is Enlightenment?* (1784) Immanuel Kant says, "Nothing is required for this enlightenment, however, except freedom; and the freedom in question is the least harmful of all, namely, the freedom to use reason publicly in all matters."[13] Simple as Kant makes this sound, he also knew it was far from easy. Enlightenment isn't just about living in a society in which one is free to think for oneself and speak one's mind, but about having the courage to do so regardless of the society and circumstances one is in:

> Enlightenment is man's emergence from his self-imposed immaturity. Immaturity is the inability to use one's understanding without guidance from another. This immaturity is self-imposed when its cause lies not in lack of understanding, but in lack of resolve and courage to use it without guidance from another. *Sapere Aude!* "Have courage to use your own understanding!"—that is the motto of enlightenment.[14]

It was this Enlightenment principle that inspired the framers of the Declaration of Independence, U.S. Constitution, and Bill of Rights, however imperfectly their grand aspirations have oft been achieved or resisted. It is also the principle upon which American Unitarianism was founded during its 18th century inception in Philadelphia, where the first American church to call itself *Unitarian* was founded in 1796 by Joseph Priestly, a friend of Benjamin Franklin, and whose theology made such an impression on Thomas Jefferson that he once said, "I trust there is not a young man now living in the United States who will not die a Unitarian."[15] Jefferson's prediction fell far short of coming true, yet the Enlightenment values of freedom, tolerance, reason, science, humanism, and that which Kant considered its chief quality, the courage to dissent, have, until lately, been integral to the very definition of American's most liberal religion. I know of nowhere this is more succinctly illustrated than in the 1888 bylaws of the congregation I humbly serve, the Unitarian Universalist Church of Spokane, founded as the Spokane Unitarian Society in 1887, and where Religious Humanism was born only a few years later, in 1911:

> The authority of its belief is reason, the method of finding its beliefs is scientific. Its aim is to crush superstition and establish facts of religion." [And its] "First principle is freedom of opinion and is subject to no censure for heresy.[16]

It is difficult to imagine that 133 years later I would be excommunicated from the community of Unitarian Universalist ministers for writing and freely distributing a book of dissenting essays at the Unitarian Universalist Association's 2019 General Assembly. Although I expected some backlash, given that such backlash was essentially what I was writing about, I could not have imagined how explosive my little book would become only a few short hours after I began giving it away: not among members of this venerable tradition, the most liberal religion in human history, who barely had enough time to read past its cover. I managed to hand out less than 200 of the 750 copies I had planned to give away before I was confronted by five members of the Assembly's so-called Right Relations Team and, before the day ended, was instructed not to return by one of the event's Co-Moderators.

During the following twelve months I would be publicly condemned by hundreds of my colleagues, fired without cause or explanation as an adjunct professor at Meadville-Lombard Theological School, censured by the Unitarian Universalist Ministers Association, learn that top leaders in the UUA had conspired with some in my own congregation to help remove me from my post, and, finally, have my professional credentials removed by the

UUA's Ministerial Fellowship Community—excommunicated from the professional community of my peers. For many, this astonishing reaction to *The Gadfly Papers* proved its points far more than reading it could have and made its impact far more potent than I could have hoped. This soft book banning, if not burning, and the immediate condemnation and year-long harassment of its author put *The Gadfly Paper's* on Amazon's bestseller list at least twice, albeit in a very niche market. Not bad for a hastily written collection of a few self-published essays.

Tragically, its meager success only proves how immovable this once noble steed has grown, and how unenlightened has been Unitarian Universalism's descent into darkness, proven by its absolute intolerance of dissenting voices. If "Have courage to use your own understanding!" is the motto of Enlightenment, then its opposite, the endarkening of this light, is the squelching of such courage by the authorities—in this case by the leadership of the Unitarian Universalist Association and the Unitarian Universalist Ministers Association. How far they have fallen from Kant's Enlightened leadership standard:

> A prince who does not find it beneath him to say that he takes it to be his duty to prescribe nothing, but rather to allow men complete freedom in religious matters—who thereby renounces the arrogant title of tolerance—is himself enlightened and deserves to be praised by a grateful present and by posterity as the first, at least where the government is concerned, to release the human race from immaturity and to leave everyone free to use his own reason in all matters of conscience.[17]

Everywhere we turn today we hear the endarkened commands to keep quiet, to go along, to be frightened, to help condemn others or risk being condemned ourselves. "But on all sides I hear: 'Do not argue!'" Kant laments. "The officer says, 'Do not argue, drill!' The tax man says, 'Do not argue, pay!' The pastor says, 'Do not argue, believe!'"[18] I am not such a pastor. I am a gadfly that has yet to bite off more than it can chew.

---

[1] *Apology* (pp. 11-12). Kindle Edition
[2] Grayling, A. C,, *The History of Philosophy*, Penguin Press, New York, NY, 2019, p. 243.
[3] Russell, Bertrand, *The Wisdom of the West*, Crescent Books, Inc., Rathbone Books Limited, London, 1959, p. 10.
[4] Grayling, ibid., p. 3.

[5] Ibid., p. 131.
[6] Russell, Bertrand, ibid., p. 14.
[7] Ibid., p. 170.
[8] Tarnas, Richard, *The Passion of the Western Mind,* Ballentine Books, New York, NY, 1991, 1993, p. 209.
[9] Ibid.
[10] Pico della Mirandola, Giovanni, *Oration on the Dignity of Man* (1496), Optimist Books by Optimist Creations, Kindle Edition, 2018.
[11] Grayling, ibid., p. 211.
[12] Spinoza, Baruch, *Tractatus-Theologico-Politicus* (1670).
[13] Kant, ibid.
[14] Ibid.
[15] Robinson, David, *The Unitarians and the Universalists*, Greenwood Press, Westport, CT, 1985, p. 23.
[16] McDowell, Esther, *Unitarians in the State of Washington*, Frank McCaffrey Publishers, 1966. p. 97.
[17] Ibid.
[18] Kant, Ibid.

BANISHED

> **Ban** *verb*
> **banned; banning**
> *transitive verb*
> 1: to prohibit especially by legal means
> // ban discrimination
> // Is smoking *banned* in all public buildings?
> also: to prohibit the use, performance, or distribution of
> // ban a book
> // ban a pesticide
> —Merriam-Webster Dictionary

ON SATURDAY, JUNE 22, 2019, the day after I began and was soon prevented from giving away *The Gadfly Papers* and had been asked not to return to the annual General Assembly of the Unitarian Universalist Association, an email was sent out, signed "Susan FG & Carey," the Association's President and Executive Vice President:

> Note that there have been several rumors that we have banned Rev. Eklof from GA—this is not accurate. The Board and GAPC said that he may be present at GA as long as he is willing to engage in a covenanting conversation, which he declined to do.

According to both its common and lexical definitions, the word "banned" means to be prohibited from being somewhere or doing something, including, as Merriam-Webster says, "to prohibit the use, performance, or distribution of. . . a book." Even if it were true that I was only conditionally instructed not to return does not change the fact that I was *banned*. Saying otherwise is analogous to claiming, "We did not use corporal punishment: we only swatted the child's bottom for refusing to obey." The fact remains, on Friday, June 21, 2019, I began distributing a book written *for* Unitarians that I gave *to* Unitarians at a meeting *of* Unitarians, an action for which I was officially asked not to return. In other words, I was banned.

Around 7:30 that evening, having spent about six hours managing to hand out less than a couple hundred copies of *The Gadfly Papers*, I exited the GA's tradeshow intending to head home for the night when a UUA staff member approached me in the event's common area and said, "The Right Relations Team would like to talk to you. Are you available?"

"Sure," I said.

After communicating briefly on a two-way radio, the individual asked, "Do you know where the Right Relations Team office is?"

"No," I said. "But I'm not going to 'the office.' If someone wishes to speak with me, please tell them they can meet me here. I'll wait."

After a few minutes, I was met by four individuals who briefly introduced themselves and then asked if we could find a quieter setting. Fortunately, two of my church members were nearby and willing to accompany me as I was ushered to a seating area just outside "the office." After a moment, another member of the team exited the office, sat down next to me, and remained completely silent during the entire meeting. Another, by contrast, was noticeably and unusually hostile from the moment we sat down, sneering and gazing at me with the appearance of contempt. Like the others, except the participant who did not speak, he kept complaining about what I did *not* discuss in my book, some of which I had. "You haven't read my book, have you?" I asked this after he accused me of not addressing systemic racism.

"I've read about half of it," he confessed, which was half more than all the others, who admitted they hadn't read it at all, although they all agreed it had caused terrible "harm."

"Look," I said, "I make it a point not to respond to criticism for things I did not say. Why don't we talk about what I did say?" Such a conversation was not possible since, for the most part, they were unfamiliar with the book's contents. It was, thus, hard to imagine what their reasons were for the confrontation. How could those claiming to be Unitarian Universalists confront a minister about what he had written in a book, let alone a book they had not read? It seemed unthinkable.

Nevertheless, they repeatedly claimed that my book had caused great harm and hurt people, a book that had only made its appearance a few hours earlier. In a moment of frustration, recalling all I had written in *The Gadfly Papers* about concept creep (that simply hearing ideas we disagree with is harmful) and safetyism (that we must be protected from hearing harmful ideas), I snapped back, "Show me the blood!" It was not my finest moment, and there were similar *faux pas* from others, but, after a couple of necessary apologies, the near hour-long meeting remained cordial, though it was ultimately unproductive.

I was particularly bewildered by the angry man, since he had introduced himself as a colleague, yet his continued behavior seemed uncharacteristic of a Unitarian Universalist minister who should, presumably, exhibit better emotional control and thoughtfulness. As it turned out, he later wrote a brief article about the incident for his congregation's newsletter, indicating his behavior had all been part of a disingenuous act:

> My role was, as it is, to be terribly hurt by Eckhoff's accusations, in part because they ignore the systemic oppression of people of color and the G, L, B, T, Q community in America and also due to the significant efforts at normalizing racial equity I witnessed in ▮▮▮▮ prior to my arrival in ▮▮▮▮.

In addition to misspelling my last name and grossly mischaracterizing the content of my book, this struggling thespian, who seemed to portray being "terribly hurt" as anger, also thanked the individual who invited his participation for "sizing up the situation, and knowing that I might be an appropriate older, white male who disagreed sharply with the views shared by Eckhoff." (This was *a priori* knowledge, given he hadn't read any of my book at the time of the request.) He then concluded his account by wrongly claiming, "I note that this minister has already withdrawn from the UU Ministers Association and was unwilling to enter into further discussions with representatives from the UUA." This final claim was more inaccurate than his misspelling of my name. At the time this article was written, sometime in July of 2019, I was still in good standing with the UUMA and remained a member for nearly a year before being excommunicated in June of 2020.

None of this agrees with my understanding of "right relations," but here I want to discuss the fallacies associated with this ongoing claim that I was not at all banned, fired, condemned, censured, and excommunicated because of my book, but because I have "refused to engage." As this work proceeds, I will provide ample evidence proving it was my inquisitors who would not "engage" by failing to answer my repeated questions or respond to my concerns about their draconian reaction to my book. To this day, nobody from the UUA or UUMA has ever requested a conversation with me about the concerns expressed in *The Gadfly Papers*.

I was summoned to a 7:00 AM meeting only hours after I began distributing the book, to discuss the "disruption" it was causing. I was "invited" to let them guide me in a "process of public restoration," in the very same public letter where they had wrongly accused me of being a white supremacist. And I was commanded to attend a tribunal facilitated by an individual who had publicly condemned me and my book on the day of its debut by calling it the "dissemination of racism, ableism, and the affirmation of other forms of oppression, including classism and homo- and transphobia." I'll have more to say about this later, but now I wish only to draw attention to the straw man fallacy of this repeated attempt by the UUA and UUMA to justify its own bad behavior. It sounds much better, after all, to say, "He refused to engage," than to admit, "We've banned a book and condemned its author."

The most obvious flaw with their claim is that it is *ex post facto* (after the fact). The assertion that their punitive behavior was a consequence of my refusal to engage begs the question, engage about what? My book? Certainly not. Again, nobody from the UUA or UUMA has ever asked to "engage" with me about the concerns expressed in The Gadfly Papers. To the contrary, asking me to enter into a process of restoration, or to agree to their interpretation of an unspecified covenantal agreement, or to attend a trial prosecuted by an individual who has already declared my guilt, leaves no room for a reasonable or fair conversation.

Furthermore, to claim I "refused" indicates that these individuals and entities believe they had some authority to rightfully require my presence to begin with. They did not. I am both an American citizen, utterly free from the demands of authoritarian religious leaders, and a Unitarian Universalist minister with a free pulpit in an autonomously governed congregation. To say I "refused" is hubris. I simply chose not to recognize such false authority, which is both my right and my responsibility. It would be unkind and unethical for me to contribute to their authoritarian delusion by respecting impotent summons, tribunals, and inquisitions.

Additionally, the word "engage" gives the false impression that UUA and UUMA leadership was asking me to enter into a mutually beneficial dialogue in order to better listen to and understand each other. But, again, I have yet to be invited by them to discuss the concerns and contents of my book. The "engagement" they claim the right to expect was requested in the context of banning, censuring, and investigating me. It would thus seem what they really mean by this euphemism is that I refused to "obey." If so, they would be correct. As an Enlightenment thinker, I would consider it an act of cowardice to bolster a presumption of authority where there isn't any.

Shortly after arriving home the evening of the June 21st, following my meeting with the Right Relations Team, I received a phone call from a member of the General Assembly Planning Committee informing me of a policy prohibiting the distribution of materials beyond one's designated booth in the Exhibit Hall. Although this policy seemed unusual, given my past experiences at these assemblies, I respectfully agreed to abide. Before completing that call, I received another from a restricted number just after 9:00 PM. It was a GA Co-Moderator informing me, "I and a member of the UUA Board of Trustees and a member of the Right Relations Team need to talk with you about the disruption your book is causing at GA. We've set aside a time at 7:00 AM. Can you be there?"

After dozens of thoughts raced through my head in a nanosecond, I replied, "No. I'm not going to come to that."

"What?" The Co-Moderator asked, with incredulity.

"No. I'm not going to attend that meeting," I repeated.

"Oh. Then I'm going to have to ask you not to return to GA."

"Okay," I said.

"I respect that." The Co-Moderator said, bringing an end to our short conversation.

The next day, Saturday, June 22, 2019, after word got out that I'd been banned from the General Assembly because of a book, the UUA leadership needed to do some quick damage control in light of how poorly such behavior reflects upon what is supposed to be the world's most liberal religion. Hence the aforementioned email claiming, "The Board and GAPC said that he may be present at GA as long as he is willing to engage in a covenanting conversation." I'm not sure when the Board and the GA Planning Committee met to decide this, before or after I had already been banned the night before. Nor do I know to whom their decision was conveyed, but I know it wasn't conveyed to me. Again, about an hour after having been confronted by five hostile members of the GA's Right Relations Team, I received a call summoning me to another meeting first thing in the morning to discuss the "disruption your book is causing at GA." If it had been an invitation to have an honest, rather than reactionary and authoritarian, conversation about my concerns, I would have been happy to participate, but that would require those wishing to discuss it to have taken the time necessary to read it. Instead, the President and Vice-President of the UUA issued an untrue statement claiming I would not "engage" or enter into this innocuous-sounding "covenanting conversation," which, I would guess, meant I would not be allowed to return until I agreed to stop handing out my book.

Later that day, toward evening, I noticed I had received a voicemail from a restricted number. "Hey, this is the Co-Moderator again," the message said, "just checking in to see how you're doing and remind you you're welcome back to GA if you're willing to attend a meeting to reenter into right relations and covenant." The tone was more conciliatory than the night before and I immediately noticed the messaging had changed. Now, instead of summoning me to present myself before the church authorities to "discuss the disruption your book is causing," I was being invited back "into right relations and covenant." Nevertheless, given that the number was restricted, I couldn't have responded if I had wanted to, which I did not. For I do not believe it is I who was or am "out of covenant," but those who have taken punitive, public, and panicked measures to silence anyone demonstrating the ability "to use one's understanding without guidance from another," especially their guidance. Given that there was no means for me to respond to this restricted call, furthermore, I presume the message was left for show, *ex post facto*, so they could feel more authentic regarding the story they had quickly concocted to coverup their banning of a minister for writing and distributing a book.

On Sunday morning, June 23, 2019, the final day of the General Assembly, only hours before its conclusion, I also received an email from the same Co-Moderator, time-stamped 7:33 AM, stating:

> This email is to reiterate what I said to you via phone yesterday: you are welcome to participate in General Assembly events after you enter into an agreement with us about how you will uphold the covenantal commitments of our community at GA. This will require discussion and agreement with me as the Co-Moderator, and with representatives from the GA Planning Committee, about engaging at GA in keeping with values and purposes of the GA gathering. Please inform us in advance if you plan to return to the convention center or other GA spaces; respond to this email with the time and location that you will arrive, and we will meet you there so that we may seek to reach agreement.

This 11th hour PR effort is misleading from the start, given its suggestion the Co-Moderator was reiterating something "said to you via phone yesterday." I presume this refers to the previously mentioned voicemail left by a restricted number that I could not have possibly responded to. Yet, for anyone seeing this email, it would appear as if an actual conversation had transpired between us.

I also received a call that same morning from a member of the Unitarian Universalist Ministers Association's Board of Trustees asking me to meet with her and two additional Board members. When I explained I had been asked not to return to GA, she proposed we meet someplace other than the convention center. I expressed reluctance since I did not yet have a Good

Officer (a formal term referring to a trusted colleague I've chosen as a source of support). When she explained that her invitation was merely informal, I responded, "I'm still not comfortable meeting without an advocate. I wrote a book and gave it away. People can choose to read it and agree or disagree."

"I hear it's hate-speech," she then admitted, although she confessed not even having seen the book.

That was enough to solidify my decision not to attend such a meeting without representation, informal or not. Later that same morning, I received another call from a staff member of the UUA offering to speak to me as a concerned colleague. The individual advised me not to attend any meetings without a Good Officer and said it had been a mistake to have met with the Right Relations Team to begin with. This individual then advised me to establish a Good Officer as soon as possible and that it might even be wise to obtain an attorney.

Since these events, UUA and UUMA leaders have continued to perpetuate the false story that I had been asked not to return to GA because I refused to enter back into covenant. In the Fall 2019 *UU World* magazine, a brief article entitled, "Book Controversy," quotes UUA Executive Vice President Carey McDonald stating: "We asked Rev. Eklof to enter into an agreement with event organizers about how he would engage with our gathered community, which he declined to do, and we asked him not to return until he was willing to make such an agreement." As you can see above, all such communications were indirect and *ex post facto*. No such conversation ever took place between me and any representative of the UUA or GA Planning Committee.

This same propaganda piece concluded by stating, "Eklof's book drew criticism from DRUUM (Diverse Revolutionary UU Multicultural Ministries), the people of color and indigenous chapter of the UU Ministers Association, several hundred white UU clergy, and the board presidents of LREDA (Liberal Religious Educators Association)," but makes no mention of the numerous other Unitarian Universalist ministers and members who share my concerns and have written the UUA in support of me and my book. To be so blatantly propagandistic and unfair is as un-Unitarian and illiberal as is any of the unsavory conduct exposed thus far. As we proceed, we shall see similar inconsistencies, as well as a chronic return to the absurd "refusal to engage" straw man argument that was also used to justify my excommunication an entire year after the *Gadfly* affair began.

In addition to showing a lack of integrity by UUA and UUMA leadership, who would have had to admit they condemned me because of my writings, the misleading and unfair use of their propagandistic *UU World* magazine to discredit me, while prohibiting my name from being mentioned in its pages or the publication of letters from those who share my concerns, has not been without some success in shaping the narrative throughout the Association. For instance, an October 30, 2019, post from a colleague to a listserv of other Unitarian Universalist ministers, states, "Despite numerous invitations from PNW ministers, UUA and UUMA staff, Todd refuses to meet with anyone who doesn't praise his text." In addition to violating the UUMA's ethical standards by making public statements critical of other UU ministers, this statement fails to note that I have not communicated with this particular colleague in many years. Other than hearsay and reading the numerous falsehoods repeated by the UUA and UUMA, this individual could have no idea whom I have and haven't "engaged" with about *The Gadfly Papers*, nor the nature of any of the, so-called, "invitations" I've received.

To repeat, I have been asked to attend meetings in which my guilt had already been decided, including a meeting to discuss the "disruption" my book was causing and a tribunal conducted by those who had already publicly condemned me, and I have been asked to allow my inquisitors to "guide" me in a public process of restoration. To date, however, no one from the UUA or UUMA has ever asked me to attend a meeting to discuss the concerns my book raises. As an Enlightenment thinker who is part of what, until recently, has been an Enlightenment-based religion, it would be unethical for me to comply to such despotic demands. "Immaturity," to repeat Kant, may be "the inability to use one's understanding without guidance from another," but the converse is also true, "Nothing is required for this enlightenment . . . except freedom; and the freedom in question is the least harmful of all, namely, the freedom to use reason publicly in all matters."[1]

---

[1] Kant, ibid.

CONDEMNED

We are all heretics in the eyes of those who do not share our views… Let us be tolerant towards one another and let no one condemn another's belief.

—Sebastian Castellio

IN 1553, SPANISH THEOLOGIAN Michael Servetus was executed by the religious authorities in Geneva, Switzerland, for writing a book questioning Trinitarian doctrine. Reformer John Calvin personally tried and convicted Servetus for this heresy, as well as for questioning infant baptism and the deity of Christ, sentencing him "to be bound and taken to Champel and there attached to a stake and burned with [his] book to ashes."[1] After his martyrdom, Servetus became known as the founder of Unitarianism, which eventually gained favor in Eastern Europe: enough that, for the first time in history, it became officially sanctioned when Hungarian King John Sigismund Zápolya embraced it as his kingdom's official religion during the Diet of Torda in 1567. A year later, he and his Unitarian Bishop, Ferenc Dávid, issued the Edict of Torda, considered the first of humanity's laws protecting freedom of conscience and assuring religious tolerance:

> . . . in every place the preachers shall preach and explain the Gospel each according to his understanding of it, and if the congregation like it, well. If not, no one shall compel them for their souls would not be satisfied, but they shall be permitted to keep a preacher whose teaching they approve. Therefore none of the superintendents or others shall abuse the preachers, no one shall be reviled for his religion by anyone, according to the previous statutes, and it is not permitted that anyone should threaten anyone else by imprisonment or by removal from his post for his teaching.

As events surrounding *The Gadfly Papers* have shown, the once liberal religion has fallen tragically far from this original vision of freedom and tolerance, with its leadership now behaving more like those Medieval inquisitors who put Servetus to death than like the mature society Sigismund and Dávid fashioned by promising to "prescribe nothing, but rather to allow men complete freedom in religious matters." This would be troubling enough were it not for hundreds of Unitarian Universalist ministers who have also re-embraced the primitive religious habit of condemning and ostracizing heretics and dissenters. Only instead of crying "heretic," "witch," or "demon," today they deem everyone and everything they hope to squelch, "racist," "white supremacist," "homophonic," and the like.

On June 22, 2019, less than 24 hours after I began distributing *The Gadfly Papers*, a public letter was issued by the UUMA People of Color and Indigenous Chapter, signed by 39 individuals, 28 of whom are Unitarian Universalist ministers: most of the rest were aspiring to become so. The letter begins, "As we conclude a General Assembly reflecting on the Power of We, clergy of color are faced with the dissemination of racism, ableism, and the affirmation of other forms of oppression, including classism and homo- and transphobia, in a book called The Gadfly Papers by Todd Eklof." Without ever lifting a single example from my book, the statement then insinuates that its contents violate the following UUMA guidelines:

- I will demonstrate respect and compassion without regard to race, color, class, sex, sexual orientation, gender expression, age, physical or mental ability or ethnicity. Such equitable treatment shall be extended to all to whom I minister regardless of position in the organization, including to those who may disagree with me.

- I will work to confront attitudes and practices of unjust discrimination on the basis of race, color, class, sex, sexual orientation, gender expression, age, physical or mental ability, or ethnicity, and to challenge them within myself and in individuals, congregations, and groups I serve.

Anyone reading *The Gadfly Papers* must work extremely hard to spin anything in it to support the claim it violates these guidelines, which is probably why none of its critics ever quote anything in it. My book, in fact, is not about racism, but about Unitarian Universalism and how far it has strayed from its liberal tradition and values. Admittedly, some examples of this departure, as cited in my book, involve the new UUA and UUMA's use of a cultish devotion to what bestselling author, columnist, and Columbia University professor John McWhorter has since named TWA (Third Wave Anti-Racism).

In his June 2020 *Atlantic* article, "Kneeling in the Church of Social Justice," McWhorter says that social justice philosophy has morphed into a kind of religious cult that has different methods and attitudes from those of the anti-racism waves that had previously worked well against slavery and segregation. He says Third Wave Anti-Racism focuses instead on "psychological rather than institutional"[2] concerns.

As previously mentioned, in his earlier 2018 article, "Virtue Signalers Won't Change the World," McWhorter explains, "This focus on the psychological has morphed, of late, from a pragmatic mission to change minds into a witch hunt driven by the personal benefits of virtue signaling, obsessed with unconscious and subconscious bias."[3] In his previously mentioned article, when speaking of just how widespread this "phenomenon of hypersensitivity" has already become, McWhorter states explicitly, "Unitarianism has been all but taken over in many places by modern anti-racist theology, forcing the resignation of various ministers and other figures."[4] These resignations, not to mention my excommunication, have occurred precisely because, as McWhorter succinctly says, "The new faith also manifests itself in objections to what its adherents process as dissent."[5]

Although *The Gadfly Papers* argues in favor of the "common humanity" approach to racial injustice, advocated for and practiced by Dr. Martin Luther King, Jr., it would seem anyone who doesn't accept the UUA's and UUMA's particular approach to dealing with this important matter is automatically labeled racist, presumably including John McWhorter who is among other nonwhite luminaries criticizing it. As an individual who has successfully helped to institute Restorative Justice programs and helped decriminalize marijuana, I have done more to positively impact the lives of nonwhite citizens in my communities than those using TWA, which often only makes its adherents feel better about themselves by shaming others. Contrast this with the words of Civil Rights activist Dr. Pauli Murray, who famously wrote, "When my brothers try to draw a circle to exclude me, I shall draw a larger circle to include them. Where they speak out for the privileges of a puny group, I shall shout for the rights of all mankind."[6] This humanistic sentiment, which inspired Dr. King, is contrary to the identity-based ethic now being touted within Unitarian Universalism because it divides, rather than unites, the human family.

Despite the successes I have had using this common humanity approach in helping to achieve greater racial justice, which are more fully discussed in *The Gadfly Papers*, 39 of my colleagues in the UUMA People of Color and Indigenous Chapter have publicly accused me of being a racist simply because I do not ascribe to their idea of what racial justice work should look like. If this weren't bad enough, their public statement goes on to argue:

The material in question lacks both respect and compassion, continually asserting that if people of color would only be logical, things would be different. Unfortunately, since racism is not logical, logic cannot be a primary tool in its resolution. The material goes on to single out a religious professional of color, ▮▮▮▮▮▮▮ as the cause of the problem of having to deal with racism, in a clear case of racialized bullying.

Rush Limbaugh could not have concocted such misleading spin. It's as if the authors of this letter are referring to another book entirely, making it clear that in the less than 24 hours between the distribution of my book and the issuing of their statement, they had not taken time to read, let alone process, its contents. Nowhere in *The Gadfly Papers* do I say anything asserting that people of color should be more logical, nor that things would be different if more of them were. Yet their argument that racism is not logical, therefore logic cannot be a primary tool of its resolution, is itself illogical, which I find tragic coming from Unitarian Universalist ministers who are part of a religion that has, until now, been devoted to the use of reason. It is like saying medicine is not illness, therefore, medicine cannot treat illness. Just as medicine is made to treat illness, logic exists to treat illogic.

The claim that my book is a "clear case of racialized bullying," simply because I question the argument of an individual asserting that ▮▮ rejection for a job in the UUA proves it is a White Supremacist organization, is as absurd as it is defamatory. On the contrary, I don't even mention this individual's name in the book, addressing only the UUA's uncritical and one-sided response to ▮▮ unproven accusations. Clearly this letter was not meant to be honest, but to silence and discourage dissent by immediately condemning anyone its signers disagree with, by pointing their fingers and shouting the modern equivalent of "witch!"

The statement then goes on to reject:

1. The assertion that conflict concerning racism is a problem of faulty logic and can be addressed by logic.
2. The assertion that the faithful service of ▮▮▮▮▮▮▮ is the source of the problem. ▮▮ work has been the embodied practice of our liberation. We embrace the work of ▮▮▮▮▮ and other religious educators of color with a deep respect and gratitude.
3. The assertion that changes of heart and changes of practice will leave white Unitarian Universalists with less. All of us will benefit from the healing of our movement.

If the writers of this letter were more sincere, they would have the grace to cite the instances in my book they claim make these assertions. They have not because they cannot. Not only have I not made these assertions; I fundamentally disagree with them. I do not assert that racism is a problem of faulty logic, that the individual *they* name is the source of "the problem" (whatever unstated problem they might be referring to), or that "changes of practice" will leave white Unitarian Universalists with less. Publicly condemning me, especially with made-up excuses and false witness, is the real injustice here, as well as a genuine violation of the UUMA's ethical guidelines that state:

> When speaking to or about a colleague in any venue or media, public or private, I will do so respectfully. There are times when it is necessary in the service of the greater good to name a colleague's problematic behavior, whether related to misconduct, malpractice or incompetence. In naming such behavior, I will speak honestly but not unkindly, and I will use descriptive rather than judgmental language. This means I will describe the behavior and its impact, and not engage in name-calling.

Yet the letter at hand begins by accusing me of "racism, ableism, and the affirmation of other forms of oppression, including classism and homo- and transphobia" citing no evidence, charging me with violating a professional code of conduct without providing a single example of how I had supposedly done so, then going on to condemn me for making assertions that cannot be found anywhere in my book. Their public statement can hardly be considered respectful, honest, or kind, or to be without judgment. It is, rather, based upon unsubstantiated accusations and made-up falsehoods by a group of Unitarian Universalist ministers eager to condemn and make an example of any potential dissenter, while demonstrating no apparent need for some familiarity with the minister or the material they so readily slandered.

As troubling as this statement is, however, having been signed by 39 UU ministers or ministerial aspirants, it is no more so than a second statement issued the same day, June 22, 2019, initially signed by over 300 Unitarian Universalist ministers and aspirants, and eventually by more than 500. The so-called "White Ministers Letter" begins:

> With sadness and anger, we, the undersigned, join our voices with the chorus of Unitarian Universalists speaking up to name the harm caused by yesterday's release of *The Gadfly Papers: Three Inconvenient Essays by One Pesky Minister*, written and self-published by our colleague the Rev. Todd F. Eklof and

distributed at the 2019 General Assembly in Spokane, Washington. As white ministers, we write today to make clear that this treatise does not represent us or our values, nor does it represent our vision for the ministry or for Unitarian Universalism. We deeply regret the harm this publication has already caused, and we know that this is another (intentionally provocative) incident that comes on the heels of months, years, generations of harm toward our colleagues of color. (We also acknowledge the harm in the treatise directed toward LGBTQ+ people, religious educators, people with disabilities, and others—many of whom are also people of color at the intersections of multiple identities.)

As discussed by Greg Lukianoff and Jonathan Haidt in *The Coddling of the American Mind,* this opening paragraph is another kneejerk example of safetyism and mind-reading—the notions, respectively, that words are harmful and that the woke few have the magical power to know the intentions of others based upon their color, gender, and sexuality, particularly if they are white, male, or straight, and especially if they are all three. The signers use the word "harm" four times in four sentences, without once speaking to the nature of such "harm." They then claim it was "intentionally provocative," as if to assign some malicious intention on my part. Even if this were true, and it isn't, what is the harm in writing a provocative book? Shouldn't having the courage to provoke slumbering steeds to life be praised by liberals, not condemned? My little book of self-published essays is not worthy of such praise. Had most of the signers of this second letter actually read the book and given it fair consideration, I might receive their compliment with gratitude. As it stands, however, it cannot be taken any more seriously than the rest of their letter.

I will not go too deeply into the contents of this second letter here but will include it in its entirety in the appendices of this work. Rather, for brevity's sake, I will focus on its most astonishing statement:

> We recognize that a zealous commitment to "logic" and "reason" over all other forms of knowing is one of the foundational stones of White Supremacy Culture.

It should be unnecessary to remind Unitarian Universalists that, "Humanist teachings which counsel us to heed the guidance of reason and the results of science, and warn us against idolatries of mind and spirit," is a statement that remains listed as a source of spiritual growth in the UUA bylaws. Yet, as one attorney and ACLU volunteer interested in this matter told me, regarding the blanket association of logic and reason with White Supremacy, "This extraordinary statement is one for the history books!" If for no other reason, this document, signed by over 500 Unitarian Universalist ministers, a significant percentage of all such ministers, must be considered an important historical document for containing such an astounding claim.

As you will recall, disparaging remarks regarding the use of logic were also made in the previous letter and, as we shall see in the next chapter, have been doubled down upon by the UUMA. After condemning the use of logic and reason as a foundation of White Supremacy, the letter goes on to state, "Instead of accepting the frame of Rev. Eklof's arguments and debunking them," its signers will affirm what it is they do believe. How peculiar and unjust it is to condemn a man for his writing while not taking the time to cite his arguments and debunk them! Shouldn't debunking the specific assertions they disagree with be precisely the point of such a letter?

Yet, without including more detailed explanations of their assertions, the signers affirm the following:

- White Supremacy Culture (WSC) is alive and well within Unitarian Universalism.
- We believe our siblings of color as the experts in their own life experiences.
- When unjust power structures—and those who benefit from them—are exposed and critiqued, backlash is predictable.
- Neither the perspectives espoused in this publication, nor the harmful process by which it was distributed, represent our understanding of competent, compassionate, courageous UU ministry.

While I take some issue with all of these assertions, especially as applied to *The Gadfly Papers* without the courtesy of substantiation, here I will only point out another remarkable claim that should be preserved for the history books. In the letter's explanation of its third bullet point, after claiming, "Ideas and language can indeed be forms of violence, and can cause real harm," it goes on to say, "The predictable 'freedom of speech' arguments are commonly weaponized to perpetuate oppression and inflict further harm." These statements demonstrate safetyism at is worst. By first discouraging the use of reason and logic as forms of "white supremacy," the letter sets its signers up to justify silencing anyone they disagree with by equating language to violence and freedom of speech to oppression. If they succeed in propagating this attitude throughout Unitarian Universalism, it will mean an end to the Enlightenment principles the religion is founded upon, especially those of reason and the freedom to publicly express oneself without fear of condemnation.

If the anti-intellectualism demonstrated in this letter isn't concerning enough, the fact that so many ministers and aspiring ministers signed it, signifies that troubling changes are coming to Unitarian Universalist pulpits everywhere, except for those where such change has already occurred. This may be happening because our two Unitarian Universalist theological schools, Starr King and Meadville-Lombard, are, in my opinion, demonstrating the same aversion to honest discourse, critical thinking, and challenging the presuppositions of their students that has been increasingly plaguing all of Academia since the late 1980s. This is when, as Humanities professor Mark Lilla writes, our educational institutions began training "students to be spelunkers of their personal identities and left them incurious about the world outside their heads."[7] He goes on to explain, "The more obsessed with personal identity campus liberals become, the less willing they become to engage in reasoned political debate. . . . What replaces argument then is taboo. . . . Propositions become pure or impure, not true or false."[8]

In light of this, it should not be surprising to learn of an additional letter I received less than a month after giving away *The Gadfly Papers*, this time from Meadville-Lombard Theological School, my *alma mater*, dated July 10, 2019:

> Dear Rev. Dr. Eklof and ▮▮▮▮,
>
> Meadville Lombard Theological School regularly reviews its Teaching Pastor lists and the impact of our relationships with Teaching Congregations for the benefit of our students as they discern the journey towards fellowship. While we thank you for your willingness to be a Teaching Pastor and a Teaching Congregation we have decided not to continue this collaboration, effective immediately.

Other than these two sentences, the letter was signed "sincerely" by the school's Senior Director of Contextual Ministry and copied to its President, arriving only a few days after I'd received a handwritten thank-you card from the school, postmarked June 7, 2019, exclaiming, "Meadville Lombard is grateful to have you as a teammate! Thank you for your support and your ministry." A Teaching Pastor is considered an adjunct professor, compensated with the opportunity to take classes at no charge, so I count this as a letter of termination without cause or explanation. Given there were only four weeks between the note of gratitude and my termination, during which I had released *The Gadfly Papers*, the reason is clear enough. Firing professors for writing controversial books does not bode well for the quality of education or character development that aspiring Unitarian Universalist ministers and leaders are receiving at Meadville-Lombard.

Unitarian Universalists who still believe theirs to be a religion grounded in reason, freedom, tolerance, dissent, and our common humanity should be alarmed that the current and coming wave of new ministers immersed and indoctrinated in the cultish dogma of the UUA and UUMA will be the only clergy credentialed to fill our once free pulpits. As I shall discuss later, this new wave of authoritarian ministers, who are being taught to loathe the very religion they desire to lead, is also being groomed to support the end of congregational polity and the autonomy of our congregations.

The choice now seems clear, we can either revive our commitment to the Enlightenment freedoms that have, until now, defined and sustained our liberal religion, or we can let those who have deemed themselves our new church authorities do our thinking for us. The decision should also be clear, but be forewarned, there are many in the world, including within our own congregations, who prefer the easier path of simply going along with the crowd. They will not easily tolerate those who choose the path of freedom, which is the very meaning of the word *heresy*, "to choose." So choose wisely, choose with courage, choose with your eyes wide open, but choose.

---

[1] Ibid. p. 39.
[2] McWhorter, John, "The Virtue Signalers Won't Change the World," *Atlantic*, December 23, 2019
[3] Ibid.
[4] McWhorter, "Kneeling at the Church of Social Justice," *Reason.com*, June 20, 2020.
[5] Ibid.
[6] Murray, Pauli, *Common Ground*, "An American Credo," Winter, 1945, p. 24.
[7] Lilla, Mark, *The Once and Future Liberal*, HarperCollins, New York, NY, p. 60.
[8] Ibid., 90f.

PILLORIED

Few men are willing to brave the disapproval of their fellows, the censure of their colleagues, the wrath of their society. Moral courage is a rarer commodity than bravery in battle or great intelligence. Yet it is the one essential, vital quality for those who seek to change the world which yields most painfully to change.
—Robert F. Kennedy

AS WITH THE PREVIOUSLY discussed public letters of condemnation, the letter of censure I received from the Unitarian Universalist Ministers Association, dated August 16, 2019, about two months after *The Gadfly Papers* was released, does not directly criticize anything in it, although, like the others, it damns my use of reason when stating, "We cannot ignore the fact that logic has often been employed in white supremacy culture to stifle dissent, minimize expressions of harm, and to require those who suffer to prove the harm by that culture's standards." (For the full text of this letter, see Appendix A.) Although it gives small relief to know the UUMA claims to have some concern about "stifling dissent," it only seems fair to expect my censurers to have provided examples of how my particular use of logic does what they imply. As it stands, they commit a fallacy of composition by ascribing universality to what is only particular. *Some* faulty reasoning has historically been used to justify all manner of injustice, but this cannot mean that *all* logic is unjust. One might as well assert that all ships are tools of white supremacy because some were once used in the slave trade.

Making this claim says nothing that is necessarily true about my particular use of logic, additionally committing the fallacy of affirming the consequent. The invalid argument looks like this: *Logic has been used to justify the oppression of others. Todd is using logic. Therefore, Todd is justifying the oppression of others.* If this argument were valid, it would mean logic can never rightfully be used because it always leads to the oppression of others, which seems to be what the leaders of the UUMA and hundreds of its members now claim.

The letter of censure is another instance of the anti-intellectual assault on reason coming from some in Unitarian Universalist leadership—this one from the UUMA. It is telling that none of the letters discussed so far, the UUMA People of Color letter, the White Ministers letter, nor the UUMA letter of censure, directly cite any offending statements from my book, nor point out one bad syllogism, yet all three are quick to insinuate that merely using logic and reason is proof enough of white supremacy and racism. It would once have been unthinkable that such could be asserted by so many ministers and leaders in the UUA and UUMA, but, as these documents prove, what was once incredible has become credible.

Logic has many shortcomings and, as any logician would readily admit, is not a means of ascertaining truth. It is meant, rather, only as a tool for examining the quality of our own thinking and the thinking others impose upon us. Nor is the ability to use logic restricted to people with light skin, although this suggestion has historically been a far more widespread racist trope than the startling equivalency of logic with white supremacy that has now been signed off on by hundreds of Unitarian Universalist ministers. I consider this assault on reason indicative of an authoritarian mindset that encourages and depends upon its subjects' unwillingness to think for themselves.

The censure also demonstrates safetyism by repeatedly using the words "hurt" and "harm" to describe the nature of my book and my actions, additionally stating, "The content of your book has caused great psychological, spiritual, and emotional damage for many individuals and communities within our faith." I wonder what other books the UUMA would include on this list of psychologically, spiritually, and emotionally damaging books for which their authors should be publicly censured? Or did I manage to write the very first book in history that the leaders of our liberal religion feel justified in condemning?

Although the leadership of the UUA and UUMA clearly finds *The Gadfly Papers* disagreeable, to this day they have cited nothing in it that they actually disagree with, unless we include its mere use of logic and reason. Instead, since they cannot point to any real flaws in the book, at least none worth condemning me over, they resort to diagnosing invisible harms that cannot be quantified. Simply encountering ideas that we disagree with is not enough to claim we have been harmed. We live on a planet with billions of people. The obscene expectation that anyone, any group, or any community has a right not to hear ideas that upset them seems extremely narcissistic, if not solipsistic. As the former dean of Yale Law School, Anthony Kronman, says of college students in *The Assault on American Excellence,* "Although their private feelings and personal experiences may *always* be expressed and should *always* be given a hearing, they are *never* an authoritative basis for deciding any question at all."[1]

To further suggest it is intolerant simply to disagree with persons belonging to marginalized groups does deny their humanity by considering them omniscient. Fallibility is among the many qualities that are indicative of our common humanity. All of our ideas are imperfect and inadequate, mine included. Disagreeing with persons who have been oppressed does not automatically make us intolerant; but being afraid or unwilling to do so denies them the fullness and richness of their humanity.

Despite our postmodern milieu, truth cannot be culturally relevant nor determined by identity. We may all experience truth subjectively but that does not make all truths equal, nor truth an issue of equality. It is not ethical, let alone possible, for the UUA or UUMA to erect ideological barricades around marginalized groups to protect their ideas and beliefs from criticism or from simply being exposed to different ideas outside those invisible fences. Nor is the converse possible, to prevent those on the outside, no matter their skin color nor the historic dominance of their ethnicity, from being influenced by the brilliance of those now segregated anew under the deceptive guise of diversity and multiculturalism.

The letter of censure goes on to imply that by simply writing a book that the authors of the letter disagree with, I have violated the UUMA ethical code of conduct requiring ministers to express:

- Honesty and diligence in our work
- Respect and compassion for all people
- The work of confronting attitudes and practices of unjust discrimination on the basis of race, color, class, sex, sexual orientation, gender expression, age, physical or mental ability, or ethnicity in ourselves and our ministry settings.

I would argue *The Gadfly Papers* fulfills all three of these requirements, which may be why my censurers offer no specific instances of how its contents violate them. Instead, they imply that simply to write or say anything others might disagree with, especially those who have been historically discriminated against, is automatically to be dishonest and without compassion. Clearly the UUMA is now interpreting its code of conduct to mean that ministers must keep their controversial opinions to themselves at all times, so as not to risk hurting anyone's feelings. This would end our hundreds of years of commitment to freedom of the pulpit. In the UUA, "harm" and "hurt" have become the new words for "heresy," "witch," "demon."

Instead of these appellations, they now shout, "racist," "homophobe," "ableist!"

Most troubling to me, is the letter's peculiar and disingenuous attempt to express empathy for me while, at once, condemning me in a public statement they made immediately available to nearly 2,000 of my colleagues and, hence, to the entire Unitarian Universalist world. It makes me wonder if this letter was really meant for everyone else to begin with, even at my expense. It proclaims my guilt to the world, having given me no prior opportunity to respond to any grievances against me, then has the audacity to ask that I allow my kindly accusers to help fix me:

> We write this letter to ask you to seek understanding of the harm that has been done and to work toward restoration. We would welcome the opportunity to help guide and support a public process of restoration, which we expect would foster widespread learning about what it means to be a covenantal faith.

In other words, "We'd like you to publicly recant." Yet this is one of those statements that lead my critics to claim I have been unwilling to "engage" despite numerous "invitations." Were it not for a member of the UUMA Executive Team who unofficially let me know the letter of censure was coming only two days prior to its arrival, I would have been completely unaware of the matter. This is so even though, according to the UUMA's own Accountability Guidelines, I should have been informed of any grievance against me, received a copy of the grievance and official complaint, notice of the UUMA Board's intent to act on the grievance, and an invitation to attend the meeting in which the grievance is acted upon no less than thirty days after I'd been notified of it. These guidelines explicitly state, "UUMA members shall have full access and full freedom and right to respond to all evidence cited against them." With only two days' notice, I was provided no such opportunity.

I shall be forever grateful for the friendship, courage, and support of my colleague and Good Officer, Rev. Richard Davis. A Good Officer is a Unitarian Universalist Minister who upholds Unitarian Universalism's traditions and values in many ways, including being of support to specific colleagues who are facing trouble in their ministries, including grievances and tensions with other ministers or the Unitarian Universalist Association. A minister is free to choose anyone to fill this role, but Rev. Davis had been part of the official Good Officer program for more than a quarter century and was sympathetic to my views. I trusted him and couldn't have wished anyone else to serve in this capacity. His support and courage cost him many collegial friendships, assaults on his reputation, harassment from the UUMA, and, eventually, his dismissal from the Good Officer program. In a later chapter, I'll say more about the UUMA's interference and attempts to influence Rev. Davis while serving in this capacity. Here, I will only point out that he and I both wanted to provide an immediate response to the UUMA's unfounded claims in its letter of censure. But we had many questions about their process that we first needed answered, given their apparent violation of their own guidelines. Toward this end, Rev. Davis sent the following communication on September 20, 2019:

Dear UUMA Board Members,

As you may know, I'm currently serving as our colleague Todd Eklof's Good Officer. This is clearly the most challenging role I've taken on during my four terms as a Good Officer in the Pacific Northwest during the past 27 years of my ministry here.

There are many angles to this role, but for now I'd appreciate some clarification about your censure of him. I know you did not take this lightly, but I am quite confused about how this was done. If you could respond, as best you are able, to the questions below it would be very helpful.

Faithfully,

Rick Davis

The communication then listed 22 questions asking for clarification about the UUMA's process in issuing the censure:

1. What was the UUMA procedure under which this letter of censure was created? Or was it ad hoc?
2. Was the UUMA Board determination made on a purely subjective basis, or did it conform with published standards?
3. What is the intended (by the Board) effect of this letter of censure on Rev. Eklof? How is it intended/expected to affect his ministry in the future?
4. Has the UUMA issued other letters of censure (in recent years)? If so, were any of them based on ministerial beliefs?
5. The UUMA letter of censure states that Rev. Eklof has "broken covenant." Which specific elements of the covenant were the ones that were allegedly "broken?"
6. As UUMA ministerial members, are the individual members of the UUMA Board of Trustees also bound in covenant to the UUMA Guidelines?

7. Does there exist a process for revoking a letter of censure, if desired?
8. Who was the "concerned" (minister) party(s) who initiated this action (that resulted in this letter of censure)?
9. Were the minister(s)' concerns put in writing (thus converting it into a formal complaint)?
10. Did any such formal complaint describe the specific reasons for the concern and provide supporting evidence?
11. Does the "freedom of the pulpit" policy protect a minister from criticism of his/her views (from other UUMA ministers)?
12. Doesn't the freedom of the pulpit obligate UUMA ministers to speak truth as they see it? If so, was there a determination that Rev. Eklof's statements were not, in his view, truthful?
13. Did the minister(s) concerned about Rev. Eklof's views discuss their concern(s) with him (or with a Good Officer Person)?
14. Was the Continental Good Officer Person involved in this censure process? If so, how and when?
15. Was any such formal complaint provided to Rev. Eklof?
16. Was Rev. Eklof given the opportunity to examine any such complaint and respond to it?
17. Was UUMA's Committee on Ethics and Collegiality involved in evaluating any complaint against Rev. Eklof? If so, what actions did the Committee take?
18. Did the UUMA Board formally evaluate the complaint? If so, was this evaluation reflected in Board minutes?
19. Did the UUMA Board formally determine that the complaint was valid?
20. Is the UUMA Board obligated to keep its evaluation of the complaint private (except to the involved parties)? And if so, why was the censure deliberately made public?
21. In making a determination to censure Todd, was the UUMA membership involved? If so, how and to what degree?
22. Do the UUMA Guidelines include provisions that protect a targeted minister from being falsely defamed (by other ministers)? If so, how is that protection provided?

These questions represent our first attempt at formal engagement in response to the UUMA's formal letter of censure. Five days later, on September 25, Rev. Davis received a response from a member of its Board of Trustees partly stating, "I would be happy to schedule time for us to connect and talk through your questions about the guidelines, censure and policies." At this point we were clear that any response from the UUMA should be in writing, just as their letter of censure was, so Rev. Davis reiterated his request for a written response. On October 11, 2019, Rev.

Davis finally received a brief and inadequate response containing only five nonspecific and noncommittal points of explanation:

1. The letter of censure was not a membership action. . . . It is a statement based on the reality that our actions have consequences. Since it was not a membership action, which is to say Todd's membership standing in the UUMA was not impacted by this action, the Board was neither required nor advised to follow the standards laid out in the Accountability Procedures in the Code of Conduct.
2. The Board laid out in our letter of censure our views as to how Todd disregarded the Guidelines. There is no expectation nor requirement of confidentiality with a letter of censure within our documents, and others that have been made from various bodies of the UUMA have been both public and private.
3. Each Board of Trustees carries the responsibility of interpreting the covenant to the best of their collective wisdom, and hopefully does so with integrity and faithfulness. We have done our best to do so in this case, and will continue to do so going forward.
4. We are intentionally working towards being an actively anti-oppressive, anti-racist faith as a whole, and as an association, this work is part of our mission. . . . I understand that it is different, it might not feel equitable, and that it seems as though the ground is shifting. It feels that way because the ground is shifting. And we are committed, as leadership, to doing our best to support that shift.
5. In reviewing your questions, it appears to me that several of them could be answered through a close reading of our governing documents, including the Bylaws and Constitution of the Unitarian Universalist Ministers Association and the UUMA Guidelines for the Conduct of Ministry. All of these are available on UUMA.org.[2]

We were obviously dissatisfied with these responses since they didn't begin to directly address our stated concerns and questions. On the contrary, they ludicrously claimed their letter of censure didn't impact my standing in the UUMA, that they had no obligation to keep the censure confidential (although their Code of Ethics stated otherwise), that it was their job to "interpret" the meaning of the covenant they claimed I broke, and that they are taking Unitarian Universalism in a new direction requiring everyone to embrace their particular anti-racism philosophy whether they like it or not. They then finished by telling us to find our own answers online. Less than two weeks later, on October 18, 2019, I received a phone call from a UUMA Trustee informing me she understood how I might have missed the Board's invitation to dialogue because of the way the letter of censure had been phrased. I responded the next day via email stating I was not comfortable having informal conversations or meetings until our written questions regarding the formal letter of censure were addressed in writing. Because my letter of censure had been so widely dispersed throughout the Unitarian Universalist community, we wanted the UUMA Board of Trustees to explain its actions in a way that could likewise be publicly shared.

A few weeks later, in early November, the UUMA Board of Trustees received a letter signed by more than sixty concerned UU ministers, including Rev. Davis. The letter states:

> We are surprised and concerned that you unilaterally chose the confounding policy of censuring a colleague's writings, an action taken without due process: a formal complaint and an opportunity to answer it. . . . Those who initiated this letter find no violation of our covenant in Todd's book, only ideas which challenge particular approaches to anti-oppression currently in favor with many colleagues.

It goes on to suggest the aforementioned letters signed by hundreds of my colleagues, along with the unfounded letter of censure, are themselves a clear violation of the UUMA's code of ethics:

> Our ethical standard is: *I will not speak scornfully or in derogation of any colleague in public. In any private conversation concerning a colleague, I will speak responsibly and temperately. I will not solicit or encourage negative comments about a colleague or their ministry.* This norm has been violated by the mass letters and your circulation of them. They were violated in subsequent online conversations in which, for example, Todd was compared to the Nazis at Charlottesville. UUMA moderators refused to intervene in these attacks on Todd and on anyone who defends his right to speak, as they normally would do in *ad hominem* attacks. Many signatures on the letters and on online attacks are coming from colleagues who have not even bothered to read Todd's essays.

The letter concludes with a specific request:

> We ask you to engage with Rick Davis, Todd's good officer, along with a group of other experienced parish clergy of his choosing, with the goal of working in a climate of mutual respect towards a healthier stance, one that honors our collegiality and our traditions. . . . We write this letter in the collegial expectation of a quick response and the setting up of a meeting either on Zoom or face to face so that we might begin a process of reconciling our shared desire to move

toward a more equitable world and at the same time maintaining our essential value of freedom of thought.

Although this letter directly mentions hundreds of our colleagues' inappropriate reactions to my book and the UUMA's censure as reasons for its concerns, and though my Good Officer was among its signers, the letter was not signed by me, nor written on my behalf, but on behalf of its signers' expressed concern for our liberal religious tradition, especially regarding the freedoms of all Unitarian Universalist ministers. Nevertheless, on November 22, 2019, a member of the UUMA sent an email to Rev. Davis stating:

> In the recent "Request to the Board" letter that you and several other colleagues signed, Rick, one of your requests is for engagement with the Board. I'm writing tonight to underscore that the Board has desired and continues to desire the opportunity to engage. . . . Next week we expect to be able to share the Board's response to that "Request to the Board" letter. In that response, the Board plans to acknowledge that they are, in fact, eager to engage. The response will also state that they have authorized me to negotiate with you or with Todd to determine the parameters and participants of any meeting. As an act of good faith, I'm reaching out in advance of that response to let you know that meeting is a point of agreement and to see if we can begin to discuss the terms? If you and/or Todd would like to move forward in planning for a meeting, please let me know when and how you'd like to begin that work.

In response, we restated we were not going to participate in informal conversations until the UUMA Board of Trustees was willing to go on record about its processes and decisions regarding the censure. The fact that the UUMA Board of Trustees censured me for violating its guidelines under extremely dubious justifications, while ignoring the hundreds of its members who very clearly violated those guidelines, while themselves having violated their own rules, required a formal and public explanation, which, to this date, has not been provided by an organization that routinely expresses how much it "has desired and continues to desire the opportunity to engage." A formal written response to our original questions was the parameter we repeatedly set before any other "engagement" could occur involving myself and my Good Officer. The request the UUMA had received from more than sixty of my colleagues was that they engage with Rev. Davis and "other experienced clergy of his choosing." Their response seemed like another attempt to lure me into an undocumented and private conversation about a matter they chose to document and make public.

About this time, an attorney familiar with Unitarian Universalism became interested in the matter and agreed to send a formal letter to the UUMA Board of Trustees requesting a response to questions similar to those Rev. Davis and I had been asking for several months:

> Please be advised that Rev Dr. Todd Eklof has asked me to review the strictly legal and contractual due process requirements the UUMA must follow prior to any formal member discipline such as a public letter of censure. This is without regard to the subject matter of the underlying issue.
>
> Specifically, under the UUMA Code of Conduct the "Accountability Procedures" outlines a formal structural due process. After the initial informal steps of GOP involvement, the formal steps begin. To initiate my review, I hereby request copies of the following written documents as required under the UUMA "Accountability Procedures":
>
> 1) The written letter of complaint to the CEC,
>
>   > "…fully specifying the nature of concern making it a formal complaint."
>
> 2) If different, the written "formal grievance" the CEC forwarded to the UUMA Board of Trustees pursuant to CEC Option 4.
>
> 3) Pursuant to UUMA Board Rule 3 a copy of the written "intent to act" that must be sent more than 30 days prior to the UUMA's meeting.

The letter was responded to nearly two months later on January 29, 2020:

> Dear ▮▮▮▮▮,
> This is in response to your December 10, 2019, request for certain UUMA documents regarding Rev. Dr. Eklof. As is apparent from the language of the letter we sent to Rev. Dr. Eklof dated August 16, 2019, that letter was not written in response to adjudication of a specific complaint. The UUMA Board was instead responding to the groundswell of concern that had been expressed by many UUMA members, as well as affiliated organizations.
> The Board is not attempting to resolve a formal grievance, but rather inviting Rev. Dr. Eklof into a religious process of covenantal repair. We have extended repeated invitations to conversation to discern together a way forward that allows for us to come to a shared understanding and a pathway to restoration.

It is the Board's responsibility to uphold the Mission, Vision and the Code of the UUMA. After careful, prayerful discernment, we concluded a private formal reprimand was inadequate, both in response to the actions he took, and in the context of the public outcry from UUMA members.

As we are not following a formal structural grievance process, we are not including the documents you identified/requested. We remain open to entering into a process of reconciliation and restoration with Rev. Dr. Eklof.

Sincerely,
The UUMA Board of Trustees

I must leave it up to my reader to determine if it was "apparent in the language" of the censure that it was not "in response to the adjudication of a specific complaint," or not in response to a "formal grievance," or if the UUMA has in any way "extended repeated invitations to conversation to discern together a way forward." Here I will let the somewhat exacerbated attorney's response suffice as to the inadequacy of this explanation's nebulous and unsubstantiated claims:

> It would appear that UUMA's formal position is that a nationally published formal "Public Letter of Censure" does not meet the threshold of a disciplinary proceeding.
>
> In a nationally recognized case on the subject the Florida Supreme Court held that unlike social clubs:
>
>> "...a professional organization must observe due process and fairness required by Florida law in its disciplinary proceedings, and that the Ethics Committee failed to adhere to fair standards set out in its own procedural regulations in acting against petitioner in that the Committee failed to give fair and adequate notice, failed to give notice of charges with adequate particularity, and otherwise failed to provide a fair and impartial hearing."
>
> See McCUNE v. WILSON, et. al., 237 So. 169, (1970), page 170.
>
> I assume you were advised by legal counsel whether a nationally published letter of censure met this threshold.
>
> I therefore urge you to have your legal counsel contact me directly to discuss this legal "red line". In the meantime I will advise Rev. Dr. Eklof to collect all evidence of the impact on his life this letter produced.

> Of course, since the UUMA's position is that nothing formal happened this opens the door for libel. (That Rev. Dr. Eklof is Guilty of "broken covenant", employed white supremacy logic, violated the spirit of the "Ethical Standards of our Code of Conduct", including that of dishonesty, and so on).
>
> The UUMA cannot simply avoid due process by recategorizing outside its own due process rules without entering the libel arena. . . .

To be clear, to date I have taken no legal action against the UUA or UUMA, nor against anyone else (despite online rumors to the contrary). Here the only point is that the UUMA, which claims it is eager to "engage" and has extended repeated invitations to do so, has repeatedly failed to sufficiently respond to requests for documentation regarding its processes around the censure, except to finally, and nonsensically, assert its leadership doesn't consider a letter of censure condemning a minister and his actions, sent to nearly 2,000 of his colleagues, a form of "discipline." Hence, they felt no need to abide by their own rules.

The claim it has been frustrated in its numerous attempts to "engage" certainly makes the UUMA look more innocent and open than the content of these various communications otherwise proves. The truth is, after several repeated attempts to begin such dialogue by asking the UUMA to provide answers to our bewilderment about the inexplicable violation of its own norms and procedures, it failed to earnestly and openly do so, even after being contacted by an attorney, making it impossible for us to trust we could enter into a genuinely fair and purposeful conversation—not with an entity that had already decided the purpose of such a meeting would be for them to help me repair a "covenantal" agreement I did not break.

After recognizing we would never receive a satisfactory or honest reply to our many questions, Rev. Davis finally responded to the letter of censure half a year later on January 10, 2020:

> To the UUMA Board of Trustee members (who signed the August 16, 2019, letter of censure of Rev. Dr. Todd Eklof):
>
> Most regrettably, you have failed to adequately respond to our September 20th, 2019, written requests for clarity regarding your process and explicit reasons for your public censure of Rev. Dr. Todd F. Eklof. As I now have no expectation you will provide this, I am responding as his Good Officer based upon what we now know to be true.

The entirety of this response is included in the appendices of this book. For now, after addressing the specific claims of the censure, Rev. Davis concludes:

> We do agree with you that "We understand from your book that you want to encourage robust and reasoned debate about the direction of our faith." However, your actions demonstrate anything but a willingness for engaging in such a debate.
>
> You say that you wish "to welcome everyone into this work, recognizing that our members represent a wide spectrum of perspectives, experience, readiness, and willingness to engage." Yet your actions completely and clearly belie those words.
>
> We call upon you to honor the claim you made in your letter of censure that: "We also call ourselves, as UUMA leadership, to be accountable to our members and to our covenant and values." To that end, because of the potentially broad implications of your actions regarding Rev. Eklof, we call upon you to distribute this letter to all of the UUMA member ministers (as you did in publishing your letter of censure, and your justification as laid out in your Censure Q&A). Our colleague ministers have a right to be aware of how your actions affect not just their colleague Todd Eklof, but potentially every one of them.

To my knowledge, the UUMA has neither responded to Rev. Davis, nor shared this letter with its membership.

Before concluding this chapter, you will be interested to learn that I am not the first to receive such a self-righteous and unfounded censure from the UUMA, indicating what may become a worsening pattern for UU ministers in the future. In March of 2018, Rev. Richard Trudeau posted the following on Facebook:

> A PLACE TO DISCUSS?
> I have reservations about current UU racial-justice ideology, and would like to find a place to discuss them with colleagues (of all races). I can't imagine that our moderators would allow such a discussion here. Can anyone suggest a place?
> Not intending to discuss my reservations now, but so readers will know the kind of thing I'm talking about, here are brief statements of some of them:
> 1. We use a non-standard definition of "racism" (racial prejudice + power) that, while emphasizing the crucial factor of relative power, tends to make anti-white racial prejudice invisible.
> 2. Some UU people of color who are not African-American, whose ethnic group has not suffered anything like what African-Americans have

suffered, appear to be appropriating the moral authority of African-Americans.
3. Much of our eagerness to attract African-Americans to our congregations seems motivated by white guilt.
4. The Commission on Institutional Change has called on congregations (2/10/18) to "answer the call to fund BLUU as an act of reparation for the denial of opportunities over centuries." As someone who in 1969 was present at a demonstration at the headquarters of the NY Catholic archdiocese demanding that such "reparation" be paid to African-American organizations, and who later decided it was a terrible idea, alarm bells are going off in my head.

Only days later, on March 21, 2019, the UUMA Board of Trustees met to censure Rev. Trudeau simply for raising his sincere questions about the UUA's approach to anti-racism work and asking for genuine dialogue. Although they did not distribute his censure to their entire membership, it did indicate they would discuss the matter with his regional colleagues.

Dear Richard,

At its meeting on March 21, 2018, the UUMA Board of Trustees voted to issue a letter of censure against you for conduct that violates our Covenant and Code of Conduct. Specifically we found that you violated our Covenant in two areas:

- To support one another in collegial respect and care, understanding and honoring the diversity within our association;
- To use our power constructively and with intention, mindful of our potential unconsciously to perpetuate systems of oppression;

We further determined that you also violated our Ethical Standards within the Code of Conduct:

- I will demonstrate respect and compassion without regard to race, color, class, sex, sexual orientation, gender expression, age, physical or mental ability or ethnicity. Such equitable treatment shall be extended to all to whom I minister regardless of position in the organization, including to those who disagree with me.
- I will work to confront attitudes and practices of unjust discrimination on the basis of age, color, class, sex, sexual orientation, gender expression, age, physical or mental ability, or ethnicity, and to challenge them within myself and in individuals, congregations, and groups I serve.

The board took these actions as a result of complaints made against you on Facebook and in your chapter meetings. We hope that in receiving this admonishment from your fellow ministers you may take time to reflect upon how your words have been harmful to colleagues, specifically women and colleagues of color.

This censure is a matter of counsel; it has no formal impact on your membership in the UUMA which you, of course, retain. However, please know that we will be in contact with your local chapter to ask how they will work to ensure that chapter meetings and retreats are truly open to, and minimally safe spaces for, UUMA members of all identities and backgrounds, and particularly for those with historically marginalized identities.

Signed,

The UUMA Board of Trustees

Here we see the beginnings of a pattern codified in my letter of censure the following year. Trudeau's censure, like mine, insinuates that simply raising questions about how some in our liberal religion are addressing racial equality is a violation of the UUMA's Ethical Standards and Code of Conduct. Notice, too, that the UUMA took this action against Rev. Trudeau because of "complaints made against you on Facebook and in your chapter meetings," without mentioning any formal grievances against him, or following its own guidelines requiring them to provide him a copy of such and a reasonable opportunity to reply. Rev. Trudeau asked to "engage," for which he was "admonished" and accused of "harming" his colleagues. In addition to shaming him in this way, he was further embarrassed by the promise his inquisitors would "be in contact with your local chapter" about the matter. He was shamed, demonized, and punished for seeking a collegial conversation.

Anyone who has been a Unitarian Universalist long enough will know the old joke, "How do you get a Unitarian to leave town? You burn a question mark on their lawn." It now appears the time has come to retire this one-liner, not merely because our inquisitors have likely deemed it politically incorrect, but because it has become meaningless. Tragically, the question-mark is no longer a symbol of what Unitarian Universalism stands for.

[1] Kronman, Anthony, *The Assault on American Excellence*, Free Press, New York, NY, 2019, p. 104.
[2] These statements have been slightly redacted for brevity. They can be found in their entirety in the appendices.

FLOGGED

Let me never fall into the vulgar mistake of dreaming that I am persecuted whenever I am disagreed with.
—Ralph Waldo Emerson

THE SUNDAY FOLLOWING the 2019 General assembly was my first opportunity to address my congregation about the chaos that ensued following the release of *The Gadfly Papers*. The service began with a standing-room-only-crowd and ended with a standing ovation by the great majority of those present. I had intended to follow the service by conducting an open discussion, allowing our members to say or ask me whatever was on their minds about what had happened. Earlier in the week, however, following the advice of a UUA staff member, our new Board president decided to bring two professionals from the UUA to facilitate the conversation. It was not until the evening before that they informed me I was not to attend the discussion at all, ostensibly because my presence would make "participants feel uncomfortable." I acquiesced, a choice I have increasingly regretted ever since.

This was the beginning of a year-long attempt by a handful of our church members—who blamed me entirely for all that had transpired at GA—to silence and ignore the large majority in support of me, while also working diligently to force me out. I'm confident that, had I persisted with my original plan, we would have worked through our differences and moved on rather quickly, an outcome my detractors, both within my congregation and throughout the UUA at large, could not abide. They needed the stress of a major conflict in order to succeed in getting rid of me.

Those who wanted me gone worked hard trying to convince themselves and everyone else the problem in our congregation was far worse than it was, including by making it far worse than it was. The reality is, our membership numbers increased that year, our finances remained sound, and the number in attendance during our upbeat and energetic services was up. Nonetheless, these were inconvenient realities not in keeping with the myth of a beleaguered and divided congregation in need of healing that, for nearly a year, was the only narrative officially being told. This troubling milieu was exacerbated by the UUA's interference working behind the scenes with our opaque Board leadership (though not our entire Board of Trustees) in a mutual effort to force me from my post.

Such interference began on day two of the *Gadfly* affair, the last day of the 2019 General Assembly, when a UUA staff member first began meeting with my congregation's new Board president, along with other members of our church, to discuss the matter without my knowledge. These exclusive meetings and communications continued frequently throughout the following year. I learned about them either accidentally or from one of our Board members who eventually resigned in response to the constant violation of our norms and bylaws, which he routinely witnessed and complained about. "If the Board was following procedure and conducting decision-making in open meetings, rather than executive sessions and via email, for which we have no protocol or policy, then I might be able to serve," he said. Finding his repeated efforts to reestablish transparency stymied and ignored, including during a secret Board meeting during which a UUA representative attended remotely to convince him, in his words, "to get me back in line," he found little choice but to step down.

Early on, in one of more than fifteen unannounced executive sessions held by our congregation's Board of Trustees between June 2019 and June 2020, a regional staff member of the UUA advised our Board to allow the UUA's Healthy Congregations Team to conduct an assessment of our congregation. "The purpose of the Healthy Congregations Team," according to the UUA website, "is to provide training, consultation and assessment for congregations who wish to embrace healthy communications and proactively engage conflict." This sounds innocuous enough, although I was immediately suspicious knowing it was suggested by a UUA staff member during a secret meeting that I had been intentionally excluded from, in addition to its poor timing in the immediate wake of *The Gadfly Papers* and my mistrust of the UUA in general due to its ongoing undermining of my ministry. Nevertheless, against my better judgment, I assented to our new Board president's wish to proceed with the assessment, with the understanding the assessors would focus mostly on our longstanding church systems, not on conflicts surrounding *The Gadfly Papers*, and that our congregation would be fully informed about the assessment and have a voice in whether or not to proceed with what was expected to be a large unbudgeted expense (about $6,000). Neither of my explicit requests was met, nor even brought to our entire Board's attention.

When I first met with the two assigned assessors, before they began their work, I restated my expectation that their focus would not be entirely on *The*

Gadfly Papers controversy, explaining the majority in our congregation had grown fatigued by it and were ready to move on from the matter. I also explained how valuable I believed an examination of our procedures and policies could be for us, asking specifically for guidance and alternatives to my contracted role as both Minister and Acting CEO of the church. I immediately liked the assessors and felt reassured we were all in agreement after our cordial conversation. About a month before their work was completed, Rev. Richard Davis and I began meeting with them once a week to discuss their preliminary findings. Instead, they let me know the success of their unrevealed plan would depend entirely upon me and that our congregation could not heal unless I was willing to follow their suggestions. "Are you willing to do so?" They asked.

"I'll have to wait until I know what exactly you're asking of me," I responded.

The following week, they asked if I had thought about what they said during our previous meeting. I responded with two questions. First, "What exactly do you mean by 'healing?'" Further explaining that my book, which neither had read, talks a lot about *safetyism* and how *concept creep* has changed the word "harmful" to now mean ideas that are simply disagreed with.

They responded with a question: "What does 'healing' mean to you?"

"It means being a community in which we can differ about all kinds of issues and still get along, just as we have always done."

My second question was a request for specifics. "What exactly are you asking me to do?" They responded by saying they would have specific suggestions during our next meeting.

A week later, they presented me with a list of seven recommendations that could easily have come directly from the UUA and UUMA as retaliation against *The Gadfly Papers*: 1) that I obtain a "ministerial coach," to help guide me in how I communicate with my congregation; 2) that I have professional facilitators present to help me dialogue with some members of my church; 3) that I give a sermon about "what I've learned through this process," referring to the coaching and facilitated dialogues, which my coach and others would help me write; 4) that I assist in finding appropriate "anti-racism" curriculum for our church; 5) that I bring voices into my pulpit whom I disagree with to engage in a point/counterpoint debate; 6) that I participate in a book study of the UUA's publication, *Mistakes and Miracles*; 7) that I work with my Board to develop "Intercultural competency."

This detailed list, which asks me to promote the very mindset I write against in *The Gadfly Papers*, while also requiring me to get speak-therapy from coaches and professional facilitators, stands in sharp contrast to the nondescript report the assessors presented to our entire congregation a few days later. It was so nebulous as to be unactionable. It was also heavily slanted in favor of the disgruntled minority in our congregation who were upset by *The Gadfly Papers*, many of whom wanted me gone. Their concerns and opinions dominated the report, although the assessors admitted they had not conducted any random sampling surveys of the congregation, which would have provided a statistically accurate picture of where our members were on the issue. We were simply told "to pay attention to your documents," for instance, but weren't pointed to any specific documents or to any identifiable flaws within them, not even when pressed. In fact, against my expressed request, which I was led to believe had been agreed upon, the entire report was in response to the conflict related to *The Gadfly Papers*. Its "Background" section begins:

> In June, 2019, Rev. Dr. Todd Eklof released a book entitled The Gadfly Papers: Three Inconvenient Essays by One Pesky Minister during the UUA General Assembly held a few miles from UUCS in downtown Spokane. The release of this book, which challenged some Unitarian Universalist norms and practices, was followed by controversy and conflict both within UUCS and within the denomination at large.

Staying with this topic throughout, it concludes by repeatedly characterizing ours as a congregation in need of "repair, healing and rebuilding," further putting most of the onus for achieving this on me. "The most important role within this effort will be the minister's," the report says. "In short, the minister's commitment and sustained effort toward healing, repair, and rebuilding will be essential." Knowing of the seven more specific recommendations made to me, I took this as further pressure on me to embrace a narrative I disagree with, to get with the program by accepting my mistake in writing *The Gadfly Papers*, and to begin making "sincere efforts" to make amends.

The minority determined to force me out, many of whom had not been active in our church for several years and had seized upon *The Gadfly Papers* conflict as an opportunity to have me dismissed, left the presentation feeling empowered and vindicated, while the majority present were only left confused. One Board member later stated, "This assessment is meaningless. It's garbage. It should be thrown away." His concerns, which were ignored, occurred during one of the few executive sessions I was asked to attend and are, thus, undocumented.

My Good Officer, Rev. Richard Davis, having once been part of the Healthy Congregations team, was initially in favor of the assessment, reassuring me it would be a positive experience for our congregation, although he too questioned its timing. He changed his mind upon seeing the assessors' specific recommendations for me, writing them in response, "If the HCT had come later I think the dust would have settled down a bit and we could have a clearer view of things and there would be more opportunity for dialogue. Todd and I both requested that the HCT come in a bit later—maybe early next year. Unfortunately, this request was ignored or overridden. There was a haste to 'fix' a problem when emotions were still raw."

After providing additional context that the assessors would not consider before their report was complete, including about the contents of my book, Rev. Davis further explained, "I'm providing this background so you can better understand why the recommendations you have made for Todd in his ministry in Spokane are untenable; viz., they are premised on the assumption that he is fundamentally in error. Acquiescing to these recommendations would be as though he were refuting all that he has said and done."

In my own response, I reminded the assessors:

> I was assured by my Board president prior to agreeing to the Healthy Congregations Assessment that the process and outcome would be about looking at longstanding systems and policies in our church that might be improved upon, and that it would be able to go beneath the current upset around me and my book. This was a concern I shared with you during our first conversation together and felt equally assured the current conflict would not get in the way of accomplishing this. I also expressed concern about the timing of this process for this same reason. As it turns out, based upon your recommendations, it's all about me and my book.
>
> I've also stated repeatedly that the issues I raise in my book are front and center in my ministry these days, will remain so, and that I won't stop talking about them no matter the fallout.
>
> The recommendations you've given are not conducive to this, nor do they reflect any of my initial concerns, or my ongoing concern that my commitment to restoring our religion isn't squelched in any way, and that I maintain exclusive freedom of my pulpit (which means expressing myself freely in and out of the pulpit, whether people agree with me or not).

After then stating my specific concerns regarding each of their seven recommendations, I concluded by stating:

> I know you have both intentionally stayed away from reading my book and familiarizing yourselves with the controversy around it, nobly trying to remain neutral. However, your recommendations are precisely what I would expect from UUA or UUMA officials who have read it. They also seem to favor the interests of a small number in my congregation who are emotionally upset at the expense of my wellbeing and that of our church members in general. . . . At this point, I am not able to support the results of your assessment before my congregation.

Despite my expressed sentiments and Rev. Davis's explicit request that, "In this case I think it will prove necessary to slow down, add some steps that allow for more dialogue before a report and recommendations are presented," the assessors moved forward, presenting their assessment as scheduled the following Sunday. Although the assessors were not Unitarian Universalist ministers, those who secretly suggested their involvement and ended up paying for their services were, so the outcome violates the UUMA guideline found in Section III, paragraph 5, of its Code of Conduct:

> Any minister who joins or participates in a congregation, agency or enterprise other than the one they serve, should recognize the authority other members may yield to them and exercise such influence cautiously and only as it supports the work of the current minister(s).

Immediately after their report, even our Board president approached me and apologized for the way the report was presented, understanding how embarrassed I must have felt seeing the many unfavorable and one-sided comments about my person projected before all on a large screen. Like so much else I had already endured from the UUA and UUMA up to this point, it was another public flogging—this time conducted within the halls of my own sanctuary.

To this day, as I have already pointed out several times, those seeking to punish me for *The Gadfly Papers* have been unwilling to consider its contents. This is true of those detractors both within my congregation and within Unitarian Universalism at large. The conversations I've attempted to have with some often began with them explicitly stating, "I don't want to talk about the contents of your book." This is true of individual members of my church, including our Board president at the time, who claimed to have never read it, even though it was supposedly at the heart of their concerns. This has been so of my critics in the UUA and UUMA who never mention its contents when disapproving of it. It is also true of these UUA assessors, whose ignorance of the matter only worsened the levels of confusion, anxiety, and upset in my congregation.

Although, ethically speaking, this may be the worst example of the UUA's and UUMA's outside interference with my ministry, it is not the only example of such behavior. Perhaps more egregious was the attempt by the UUMA to directly influence and interfere with the work of my Good Officer. On August 27, 2019, less than two weeks after I'd been publicly censured, Rev. Davis received the following email from one of my censurers on the UUMA Board of Trustees:

> Hi, Rick,
>
> A fellow good officer noticed your posts on the Gadfly Facebook page and emailed me concerned that you seemed to be struggling to clarify your role. I joined the group and am currently wading through. I've come across a couple of your comments so far, and I, too, think I hear some struggle??
>
> Anyway, I figured I would reach out, this time with my official formerly-known-as-continental-good-officer hat on, to request a conversation. All Good Officers wear different hats in different situations, and it is tricky to discern the role we are meant to play when we are accompanying a colleague through the accountability process. You will, of course, have to act as your conscience dictates, but perhaps it would be helpful to you to hear what I understand about the process and the most productive way for GO's to participate in it. Having counseled and debriefed many of our GO colleagues who have done this work, as well as having been in the role myself, I may be a good sounding board.
>
> This is challenging work, and these are complicated times.
>
> Yours in faith and friendship,
>
> ■

I've noticed this "hat switching" analogy is common within professional UUA culture these days, offered as cover or an excuse when someone is potentially crossing professional boundaries or engaging in conflicts of interest. As I tell my staff whenever I hear them using this metaphor, especially to those who are both employees and church members, "If you are an employee of this church, you only have one hat. You must always maintain your professional boundaries." I also acknowledge this is hard to do in work that is so intensely relational, and that we can only do our best. But claiming the magical ability to draw clear lines around one's role by predesignating oneself an employee, a church member, a colleague, a friend, and so forth, is more akin to schizophrenia than a sane response to the fuzziness of relational ministry. It's better, in my opinion, to do our best to remain professional at all times and to learn from our missteps in this "one hat" practice. In this case, the conflict of interest this individual had by interfering with Rev. Davis's role as my good officer was blatant, given that the individual had signed my letter of censure only days earlier. Simply claiming to have switched hats, as if one can draw clear lines between their own biases, emotions, and interests, is questionable, to say the least, and was most certainly inappropriate.

Of the posts to which this communication refers, Rev. Davis told me, "My posts on the Gadfly Paper FB page to which ▇ refers were simply to affirm that I support your right of conscience and free expression, that I am dismayed by the letter and the censure and exploring how to respond, and I've weighed in a couple of times when I felt it was helpful. I have also encouraged the UU lay folks to let the UUA and UUMA know of their displeasure (most folks on this page are in fundamental agreement that this whole fiasco impinges upon fundamental freedoms enshrined in our tradition. There are some very open and interesting discussions there)." Rev. Davis and I both agreed it was the UUMA that placed this matter within the public arena and it was, thus, his task to support me within that same arena, not simply before those few individuals who had violated their own rules in censuring me, thereby proving they could not be trusted to be honest and fair. He, therefore, responded to this individual accordingly:

> I appreciate you reaching out—I am not doing this without consulting others—I've chatted with two of my fellow good officers (▇▇▇ and ▇▇▇) as well as some other colleagues and I have several more conversations lined up so I can gain a broader perspective. I wouldn't so much say that I'm struggling now as in deep discernment as I proceed. This is not easy for any of us, but I am resolved to bring my best self forward and work for the good of all.

It would appear his best wasn't considered good enough. A few days later, on September 11, 2019, Rev. Davis received another communication, this time from the Board President of the UUMA:

Dear Rick,

I am writing today as it has come to my attention that you are planning to preach a sermon later this month regarding the controversy surrounding the Gadfly Papers. My understanding is that you are serving as Todd Eckloff's Good Officer. If that is correct, I'm concerned that preaching on the Gadfly conflict may compromise your ability to serve in the Good Offices role for Todd. I'd like to speak with you about this and make sure you understand current expectations of Good Officers. When might you have some time?

I'm copying ▓▓▓▓▓▓▓▓▓▓ as ▓▓ is the UUMA Board of Trustees member who holds the portfolio for Counsel and Advocacy and, in that role, works with me to oversee the ministry of Good Offices. If you like, ▓▓▓▓▓▓▓ can join us for our conversation.

All my best,

[The redacted name refers to the same individual who had previously expressed concern over Rev. Davis's handling of the matter.]

The implication in both communications, that Rev. Davis would have a conflict of interest should he publicly support me in his role as my Good Officer is ironic coming from two individuals who publicly censured me and were now interfering with and attempting to influence what he does and doesn't say. That they attempted to preempt his sermon is a further assault on the freedom of the pulpit our liberal religion has historically held as sacrosanct. Attempting to prevent him from speaking, rather than responding to anything he actually said, is another example of the fear and control motivating many in UUA and UUMA leadership these days, leading them to squelch dissent both before and after it is expressed.

Rev. Davis, furthermore, has often pointed out that he isn't defending me but rather defending his own religion and values. It should also be obvious that a minister involved in a highly controversial matter has an obligation to openly and fully discuss his involvement with his congregation. As he explained in his notorious sermon:

> I have been advised more than once by sympathetic colleagues that I am going to lose ministerial relationships because of my stand—and that news has shaken me. Yet as I ponder more deeply, I realize that if I did not speak out honestly in this matter I would become estranged from myself for not speaking out as my conscience clearly bids me do. So out of loyalty to my own

conscience, my ministerial calling, to you—the members and friends of this beloved congregation, to the heart of our free faith tradition which affirms our freedom of conscience and expression, and to my good friend Todd—this loyalty and my love for everyone compels me to speak honestly to challenge authoritarian, dogmatic trends in our association.

Only two days after giving his September 22, 2019, sermon, Rev. Davis was again contacted by the UUMA Board member who had initially questioned the way in which he was fulfilling his Good Officer role. After claiming to have read his sermon, the Board member stated:

> I am very concerned that your public statements seriously compromise your ability to fulfill that role, which would require you to recuse yourself should someone initiate the accountability process. While the letter of censure isn't the same as the filing of a formal grievance, there are bound to be some parallels. This could wind up doing Todd a major disservice.

What can only be taken as a feigned concern for my welfare notwithstanding, the continued implication that Rev. Davis has a conflict of interest, coming from someone who most certainly has a conflict of interest, is audacious. Clearly the UUMA's issue with him wasn't because he was not acting in my best interest, but that he wasn't acting in theirs. The expressed concerns were also highly speculative.

A second communication the same day, from another UUMA Board member, came in response to the 22 questions Rev. Davis had presented weeks earlier: "I would be happy to schedule time for us to connect and talk through your questions about the guidelines, censure and policies." This may have seemed like an olive branch, but, for us, it was another attempt to have an informal and, thus, undocumented conversation regarding our persistent request for a formal written response, something my public censurers appeared unwilling to do. For the record, Rev. Davis did have an informal conversation with UUMA Board members prior to giving his sermon, of which he told me afterward, "Basically, it went better than I thought. I was pretty blunt and didn't hold back."

On April 2, 2020, Rev. Davis received a letter signed by the President of the UUMA stating, "I am writing today to inform you that we are removing you from the UUMA's list of Ratified Chapter Good Officers effectively immediately." The reasons cited for his termination, from a position he had been elected to fill four times in 27 years, included having "repeatedly violated the boundaries of the Good Offices role," an accusation based upon a dubious and convenient interpretation of the Good Offices Handbook. "You have consistently and publicly advocated in support of the minister in your care, Rev. Dr. Todd Eklof, despite my counsel in November 2019 against publicly taking a position. I expressed to you in our conversation that public advocacy is inappropriate for a Good Officer and that you ran the risk, if you continued in that vein, of undermining your capacity to serve in the prescribed manner." In short, he had been warned to keep his mouth shut and, so, brought this outcome upon himself. "To be specific," the letter goes on to say, "I am aware that you have advocated in support of Rev. Dr. Eklof through your communications with and preaching within at least two congregations: the Unitarian Universalist Church of Spokane, WA and the Unitarian Universalist Church of Salem, OR."

In essence, Rev. Davis was terminated from this elected position for giving a sermon he had been warned not to give and for continuing to publicly share his concerns about the misdirection the UUA and UUMA are heading, including when speaking in his pulpit and in mine. This is so, despite the UUMA's own Code of Ethics stating:

> The history and expectation of the Unitarian Universalist movement is that ministers are free to speak the truth as they understand it. The longstanding tradition of freedom of the pulpit extends to ministers in all professional settings. This freedom applies to both spoken and written public statements.

It should also be understood that Rev. Davis's role as my Good Officer was still unofficial at the time of his termination. Recall the previous UUMA communication telling him, "I am very concerned that your public statements seriously compromise your ability to fulfill that role, which would require you to recuse yourself *should someone initiate the accountability process*." (Italics added) If, despite its persecutory behavior, the UUMA hadn't initiated any formal "accountability process" against me, it was not possible, even under their questionable interpretation of the Handbook, that Rev. Davis could have engaged in the conflict of interest he had been accused of and terminated for.

Clearly the UUMA did not want me to have a Good Officer who authentically supported me, which would have effectively left me without any kind of meaningful representation if formal accountability proceedings had been initiated, which they never were (not with the UUMA). It is difficult not to conclude that Rev. Davis was terminated because he did not toe the party line when it came to *The Gadfly Papers*. That he was repeatedly harassed and eventually fired for displaying bias by those who obviously had extreme bias and tremendous conflict of interest is confounding. Clearly the UUMA was wearing far too many hats in this matter—plaintiff, prosecutor, jury, judge, executioner, and, if they had their way, even serving as my self-appointed public defender.

As mentioned, there were also a small number in my own congregation who sought to force my dismissal, including, in my opinion, the President and Vice-President of our Board of Trustees. To do so, they exploited the COVID-19 lockdown happening at the time, which prevented our congregation, the great majority of whom continued to support my ministry, from meeting in an open forum to discuss and decide the matter. If, in the interim, they could have forced me into "binding arbitration," as stipulated in my Ministerial Agreement (contract), they could have bypassed a congregational vote of dismissal, which they surely would have lost. Before I would ever agree to such arbitration, however, they would need something to hold over my head. In this case, it was presumably a clause in my Ministerial Agreement stating:

> The Minister may be dismissed with less than ninety days notice, and without the salary, housing allowance and benefits described above, if the Minister is convicted of a felony or is found by the Board of Trustees of the Congregation to have grossly neglected or abused his/her ministerial responsibilities under this Agreement and/or to have engaged in activities that bring the Congregation and/or Unitarian Universalism into disrepute in the Congregation and/or community.

With time running out, only weeks before a congregational election (by mail-in ballot) would determine a new Board of Trustees, one of those working behind the scenes to have me removed sent out a secret survey on behalf of our church to members of the wider social justice community, asking leading questions insinuating our church might be racist. For example:

> The mission of the Unitarian Church of Spokane is to "champion justice, diversity, and environmental stewardship in the wider world." Do you believe that the church can achieve that mission if it disagrees with the concepts of white supremacy culture and/or white fragility?

And:

If the Unitarian Universalist Church of Spokane disagreed with the concepts of white supremacy culture or white fragility in its work, how would this impact your willingness to work with it?

And:

Has your perception of the Unitarian Universalist Church of Spokane changed in any way during the past 24 months?

When this clandestine effort was discovered and reproached, the amateurish survey immediately disappeared from its online interface. If this effort had proven successful, my detractors might have presented its unreliable results as evidence I had "engaged in activities that bring the Congregation and/or Unitarian Universalism into disrepute in the Congregation and/or community." Apparently, they believed I would agree to anything to preserve my three month's severance, which was an erroneous presumption to begin with.

About this same time, another member of our congregation, supportive of my ministry, wrote the UUA Human Resources department seeking clarification about the usual purpose of "binding arbitration." She eventually received a reply that seems to have unintentionally included an internal chain of communications between UUA officials trying to figure out how best to respond (or how best not to respond). For example, one individual wrote:

> My thought is to say that the uua provided the suggested framework to the board, and that we believe it best for ▇ to be in conversation with the board.... not sure who is best to te ssd pond [to respond] though?

Apparently having caught this oversight, the official reply stated:

> As ▇▇▇▇ and I mentioned, the UUA has been in conversation with the board of trustees about the arbitration process. We communicate with the board as the official governing body of the congregation. If you seek more information on the arbitration process, please contact the Spokane Board of Trustees.

More troubling than the brushoff, however, is that this wayward chain of communications also mentions that the Director of the UUA's Office of Church Finances, a staff member with its Pacific Western Region, and the UUA Executive Vice-President had all "been in conversation with the board at Spokane about this." This would indicate the UUA's secretive interference with my congregation involved its highest administrative office, which is a genuine violation of UUA and UUMA norms and rules. Such conversations simply should not have occurred without those involved having first made me aware of and included me in them. Instead of being genuinely concerned for the welfare and cohesion of the Unitarian Universalist Church of Spokane's entire congregation, I believe the UUA and UUMA were willing to sacrifice the welfare of its members in a concerted effort to rid themselves of their pesky gadfly.

Earlier in the year, on March 8, 2020, having their concerns and opinions routinely ignored (in every sense of this word) by our Board leaders (with whom the UUA would later discuss the termination of my contract), over 200 of our members signed and sent a resolution to our Board of Trustees, the UUMA Board of Trustees, and the UUA Board of Trustees, explicitly stating where they stood on the matter:

- We believe UUCS is a welcoming community, where diversity of thought, ideas, ways of being and knowing are our strengths—not a source of division.
- We view our congregation as healthy and vibrant as evidenced by active and engaged members and friends doing meaningful work, both within our cherished walls and outside in the wider community.
- We believe that the censure of ideas is antithetical to who we claim to be. We not only support our minister's right to freedom of conscience and freedom of the pulpit, on both the local and national level, we expect him or her to uphold our bylaws and principles using evidence and reason, as we each are challenged daily with our own free and responsible search for truth and meaning.
- We believe Rev. Todd Eklof acted with great courage. Whether we agree with his ideas in "The Gadfly Papers" or not, we respect his right to raise concerns and to be heard. We stand resolutely with him as he continues to suffer the consequences for taking personal and professional risks in upholding core principles of Unitarian Universalism.
- In challenging times, we will interact with each other openly and respectfully, keeping in mind our shared goals and historical values that have guided UUCS forward for more than a century.
- Lastly, and perhaps most importantly, we will continue to honor our individual freedoms even as we deeply understand that it is our common humanity, paired with rationality, that are essential to living in a sane and just world.

Regardless of these overwhelming sentiments, our local Board leaders, and the acting Nominating Team it had appointed, pulled together a slate of six new Board candidates, all of whom had expressed disapproval of me and *The Gadfly Papers*. This was the first time in my tenure at the church that a Nominating Team had not discussed its choices with me in advance. The reason there were so many vacancies is because three of our seven Board members had resigned over the course of the church year, in addition to those whose terms were ending.

In response, an informal group within the congregation put together an alternate slate of candidates for both the Board of Trustees and the Nominating Team. This was done in keeping with our bylaws regarding church elections. Of the 306 ballots returned, 60 voted in favor of the original slate of candidates. The other 250 went entirely for the alternative list. Despite those few who departed after this failed coup, we still have over 350 official members, plus over 125 friends who remain active in our mid to large sized congregation. Yet the UUA and UUMA not only discounted their interests and welfare but contributed to a year of unnecessary turmoil in this historic congregation, which is full of goodhearted souls who deserved better.

EXCOMMUNICATED

Reader! To whatever visible church, synagogue, or mosque you may belong! See if you do not find more true religion among the host of the excommunicated than among the far greater host who excommunicated them.

—Moses Mendelssohn

ON JANUARY 8, 2020, I received notice from the UUA's Ministerial Fellowship Committee (MFC) that the Liberal Religious Education Directors Association (LREDA) had filed a formal complaint against me for what I had written in *The Gadfly Papers*. The complaint was dated December 17, 2019:

Dear UUA Office of Ethics and Safety

This complaint is filed on behalf of members of the 2017-18 LREDA Board and the current (2019-20) LREDA Board against Rev. Todd Eklof, Minister, Unitarian Universalist Church of Spokane. This complaint concerns Rev. Eklof's self-published book, "The Gadfly Papers", released in the spring of 2019. In the book, his description of the events of the 2017 LREDA Fall Conference is filled with factual errors, misleading statements, and innuendos. He establishes a pattern of offering "evidence" to solely support his views by cherry picking events and quotes, and misrepresenting what people said and did. Eklof failed to demonstrate any diligence in pursuit of the truth of what happened at the conference. His conduct failed to demonstrate respect and compassion to all people, or investigate and confront attitudes and practices of unjust discrimination.

Background
In 2017, the LREDA Board and Fall Conference Planning Team brought ▪▪▪▪▪▪▪▪▪▪ and ▪▪▪▪▪▪▪▪▪▪ to be the featured speakers at the 2017 LREDA Fall Conference. Their presentation was found by the LREDA leadership to embody white supremacy and patriarchy, and the impact of their actions brought pain for conference participants of color, transgender people, survivors of abuse and others. As a result, the speakers' presentation was suspended early on the second day of the conference and ▪▪▪▪▪▪ and ▪▪▪▪▪▪ were paid in full and asked to leave.

Complaint

As author of "The Gadfly Papers", we believe Rev. Eklof's conduct violates the Ethical Standards in the UUMA's Code of Conduct detailed in the Guidelines for the Conduct of Ministry as follows:

Specific areas of concern under the UUMA Code of Conduct:
Ethical Standards

1. "I will be honest and diligent in my work to fulfill the offices of ministry according to the stipulations of my call or employment and my best professional judgment."
2. I will demonstrate respect and compassion (to all people) without regard to race, color, class, sex, sexual orientation, gender expression, age, physical or mental ability or ethnicity. Such equitable treatment shall be extended to all to whom I minister regardless of position in the organization, including to those who may disagree with me.
3. I will work to confront attitudes and practices of unjust discrimination on the basis of race, color, class, sex, sexual orientation, gender expression, age, physical or mental ability, or ethnicity, and to challenge them within myself and in individuals, congregations, and groups I serve.
4. I will not engage in public words or actions that degrade the vocation of ministry, or diminish among us the esteem of our calling.

The complaint then gives nine instances of what it calls "Evidence of Violations," all of which disagree with my interpretation of the facts I describe in *The Gadfly Papers,* but they do not dispute the facts themselves. This is so except for minor errors like stating the presenters were dismissed in the evening rather than in the early morning, and mistakenly referring to a LREDA Board member as a LREDA staff member. These are certainly regrettable errors on my part, but hardly worth excommunicating me over. Nevertheless, I stand by my research and interpretation of the events in question and welcome others who disagree to publicly dispute them. The complaint also criticizes me for not interviewing certain individuals that its issuers would have preferred, nor written what they would have preferred I say. Everyone has the right to criticize another's writings, and to dispute them, but not to pen them—a principle the violation of which reflects the core concerns spelled out in *The Gadfly Papers*.

I won't further discuss this "evidence" here but have made the bulk of the complaint available in my appendices for those interested in judging its merits for themselves. I would only point out a subtle but significant shift in the language used in the complaint from that which was used in LREDA's original explanation of the event in question. The organization's November

8, 2017, letter of explanation begins, "The LREDA Board and Fall Conference Planning Team *brought speakers to Fall Conference that embodied white supremacy and patriarchy*," (Italics added) a characterization that I am critical of in *The Gadfly Papers*. The complaint against me, however, expresses it differently: "Their presentation was found by the LREDA leadership to embody white supremacy and patriarchy." Suggesting now that it was only their *presentation* that embodies these evils sounds slightly more palatable than describing the two presenters themselves as such, but the claim, in my opinion, remains unfounded. Even so, the decision to reframe the matter in this way indicates some recognition of just how wrong the original slander was to begin with.

The complaint goes on to use language almost verbatim to the UUMA's letter of censure, claiming, in a preamble to a list of "impact statements," that my book "has caused great psychological, spiritual, and emotional damage," and lists the same ethical standards the censure accuses me of violating, also without explanation, and finally concludes with the following resolution:

> Members of the 2017-18 and the 2019-20 LREDA Boards ask that Rev. Todd Eklof be placed on conditional probation from membership in the MFC with the following conditions of probation:
>
> 1. Rev. Eklof will make a "Real Apology" (cited in ███████'s podcast originally from researchers at Ohio State University); which includes:
> a. An expression of regret:
> b. A genuine understanding of the harm done leading to an explanation of what went wrong:
> c. An acknowledgment of what went wrong:
> d. A declaration of repentance:
>   e. An offer of repair [in our case, this must include a statement of retraction];
>   f. A request for forgiveness.
>
> 2. Rev. Eklof will undergo one-on-one anti-racism, anti-oppression, multicultural training by a LREDA-approved qualified consultant at Rev. Eklof's expense for two (2) years, once a month, with assigned reading.
>
> If Rev. Eklof does not meet the condition of probation established by the Committee, we ask that Rev. Eklof be placed on indefinite suspension or removal from Ministerial Fellowship.

The arrogance and self-righteousness underlying this resolution notwithstanding, cries for an individual to repent, retract, beg forgiveness, and undergo reeducation or else be ostracized and exiled is the stuff of Medieval Catholic Inquisitions, not of Unitarian Universalism, not now, not ever. That the MFC did not reject this blatant insult to the Enlightenment principles undergirding our religion is only further proof of the concerns I express in *The Gadfly Papers*, with which they "refuse to engage." Still, I do appreciate that the complainants attempt to cite material from my book in support of their protests, though, overall, I consider the complaint to be only more evidence of my concerns: What was once the most liberal religion in human history, founded upon the principles of freedom of thought and expression, no longer allows room for dissenting opinions, and is becoming increasingly authoritarian and punitive, these stark changes being justified by a mad pursuit of linguistic puritanism and monolithic ideological expression. Rather than calling dissent heresy, they have merely substituted the word "harmful."

Many of LREDA's complaints seem but a matter of semantics, like my use of the term "witch hunt" as a section title; or calling my use of the word *segregated* "inflammatory," though I use it properly to describe intentionally separating individuals into specific rooms based on their color. Like all the other criticisms against my book, however, the LREDA complaint is mostly critical of what I did *not* do and say, rather than what I did do and say:

- "Eklof failed to demonstrate any diligence in pursuit of the truth of what happened at the conference."
- "His conduct failed to demonstrate respect and compassion to all people, or investigate and confront attitudes and practices of unjust discrimination."
- "Eklof made no attempt to investigate why the actions of the presenters had negatively impacted people of color and others."

Although I would dispute these claims to begin with, it can also be said that I failed to write about foot fungus and the mating call of the whippoorwill. Despite the official attempt to make *The Gadfly Papers* a book about racism (so its detractors can justify their swift condemnation of it without addressing its concerns) my book is about Unitarian Universalism's slide into dogmatism and ideological intolerance under the banner of a very narrow, unproductive, and cruel notion of social justice. There are many subjects my book does not address and many directions it could have branched into. The direction I took was my choice as its author. Nevertheless, what the complaint calls "factual errors, misleading statements, and innuendos" and "cherry-picking," I call interviews with three people directly involved in the matter and two public statements from LREDA representatives officially explaining the event. These public letters were well-written and concise, and left me with no need for further clarification from them.

Upon first reading the complaint, I could not imagine why the MFC didn't outright reject it as an affront to our tradition instead of letting me know they were taking it seriously, having already assigned a lead investigator who had publicly condemned my book as the "dissemination of racism, ableism, and the affirmation of other forms of oppression, including classism and homo- and transphobia." So, rather than making this latter point my first, we decided to begin by questioning the fundamental legitimacy of the complaint itself. On March 5, 2020, Rev. Richard Davis sent the following reply to the MFC's assigned investigator:

> Rev. Eklof (Todd) and I have conferred about his response to your request for an interview pursuant to the complaint against him lodged by LREDA to the MFC. Upon reflection, he finds that he cannot in good conscience agree to participate in this inquiry. Please know that his decision is based on principle and is in no way intended as a gesture of disrespect toward you.
>
> Regarding his decision Rev. Eklof writes: *With respect, investigating a minister for his writings is a violation of his rights as an American citizen and of his free pulpit. For the sake of our Unitarian Universalist tradition and the future freedoms of liberal ministers, I cannot in good conscience validate such proceedings with my participation. My book, our UU values, and the content of the complaint filed against me should be all that is necessary to put this matter to rest.*
>
> Speaking as Todd's Good Officer I must concur with him that having such investigations runs counter to the spirit of our free faith tradition.

On March 6, 2020, the MFC's Executive Secretary responded:

> I understand from your statement that you are refusing to participate in the process of investigating the misconduct charge against you. I want to be clear that refusing to participate in the initial investigation would be considered in violation of Rule 28 in the MFC Rules:
>
>> It is expected that all candidates for Fellowship and all ministers in Fellowship will cooperate with the Committee at all times. This includes, but is not limited to, responses to requests for information, provision of requested documentation,

attendance at meetings with the Committee, and compliance with any remediation and/or probation requirements. Non-compliance may be grounds for termination of Fellowship.

I wanted to make sure you were clear about Rule 28 when you made the statement quoted above and, if not, offer you another opportunity to participate in the investigation of the misconduct charge filed against you. With this in mind, please let me know by Thursday, March 12, 2020, if you wish to continue your refusal to cooperate with the MFC. I will inform the Committee of your decision for their consideration and action.

Since it was now clear the MFC was determined to continue this course of action, we decided to point out the obvious. On March 11, 2020, I submitted the following reply:

Thank you for the respectful tone of your response and for the invitation to change my mind regarding my participation in your investigation: an invitation I must respectfully decline. Since writing and giving away my book of dissenting views only a few short months ago, I have been officially banned by the UUA, publicly condemned by hundreds of my colleagues, fired as an adjunct by Meadville-Lombard Theological School, censured by the UU Minister's Association, and am now being investigated by the Ministerial Fellowship Committee.

Your investigator's initial communication to me stated "all parties will be treated fairly and with ministerial care." Yet, less than 48 hours after distributing my book, this same individual signed a June 22, 2019, public letter stating "clergy of color are faced with the dissemination of racism, ableism, and the affirmation of other forms of oppression, including classism and homo- and transphobia, in a book called *The Gadfly Papers* by Todd Eklof." My book affirms nothing of the sort!!!

Given the biased and libelous public response of the investigator the MFC has chosen to oversee this matter, perhaps you will understand why I cannot reasonably trust the MFC to be a neutral party at this time. I can only interpret this investigation as being without credibility and as another example of the authoritarian turn that has become widespread within the UUA, which I most certainly do write about in *The Gadfly Papers*.

So, for now, in good conscience and for the sake of freedom of the pulpit and the freedoms of other ministers, I cannot cooperate with or legitimize this further instance of authoritarian overreach occurring within our once free and noble liberal religion.

Therefore none of the superintendents or others shall abuse the preachers, no one shall be reviled for his religion by anyone, according to the previous statutes, and it

> is not permitted that anyone should threaten anyone else by imprisonment or by removal from his post for his teaching.
>
> Edict of Torda [1568]

Although firm in my stance, by stating "for now," my reply left an opportunity for the MFC to address my concerns about having a fair and legitimate hearing in light of the express bias of its assigned investigator. The next day I received a reply from the MFC Executive Secretary, which, terse at it was, I took as a good sign: "Todd, Well received. Peace." A couple of weeks later, however, on March 30, 2020, the MFC Executive Secretary sent another email informing me the Committee would be moving ahead with the investigation, without having addressed my stated concerns in the slightest. In other words, they "refused to engage."

> The Executive Committee of the Ministerial Fellowship Committee met last Tuesday and discussed the process thus far. Because you have been non-compliant with the initial investigation into this matter in violation of Rule 28 which requires cooperation with the Committee, they determined to recommend a full fellowship review to the full MFC at its business meeting on Sunday, March 29th. The motion passed, and it is now up to the Executive Committee to determine the scope of any further investigation, and to assign up to three people outside of the MFC to make up the investigating team. At this point, ▓▓ ▓▓▓▓▓▓ will turn over ▓ documentation to be considered by the new investigative team.

After providing a copy of the *Procedures for Review of Full Fellowship*, the communication concludes:

> I realize that this is difficult news, and I do encourage you to seek the support and counsel of your good officer, The Rev. Rick Davis, whom I have copied. If it is your intention to decline to participate in this full fellowship review, please let me know earliest. *Also, please let me know if you have any questions, which I will attempt to answer.* [Italics added]

As I see it, regardless of the stated rule, I am under no obligation to blindly obey without some response to my legitimate concerns about how such a process could possibly be fair considering it had already been tainted by the MFC's appointment of an obviously compromised investigator, not to mention others on the Committee who had also signed the public letters of condemnation. As one seasoned and respected minister, who had once served on the MFC, wrote to its Executive Secretary regarding this troubling development:

> I believed, and still believe, that the UUMA Board failed to treat Todd fairly and did not afford him due process. And when I learned that the person assigned to investigate the charge to the MFC filed by LREDA was a person who had signed what could fairly be called a defamatory letter to Todd a day after he distributed his book, I was aghast. The optics look like fairness and due process, despite that being the MFC's and the investigator's at least implicit obligation, are not being offered Eklof. It looks like the MFC (or you, if you were the person to appoint the investigator) has already determined that Eklof should be a sacrificial example. Please reconsider.

On April 23, 2020, I too responded decisively to these sham proceedings:

> I object to the MFC's decision to continue with its wrongheaded and unfounded investigation of me. It is difficult to believe there is no mention of my concern regarding the very public and outlandish bias expressed by your chosen investigator, who (quite falsely) claimed I have disseminated "racism, ableism, and the affirmation of other forms of oppression, including classism and homo- and transphobia." Unless the MFC has redefined the meaning of these offensive labels, it is unclear why I, rather than others, am being investigated for violating the UUMA code of conduct.
>
> And relatedly, why is the MFC (a separate organization) investigating me for allegedly violating the UUMA's code of conduct? This seems to be further evidence of the conspiratorial collusion occurring between the UUA and UUMA leadership to make an example of dissenters.
>
> The point here, however, is that your investigation, without question, has been tainted from its very inception. Yet the MFC has chosen to plow ahead without even addressing this disgrace.
>
> I request to know the precise nature of the "ministerial misconduct" I'm being accused of.
>
> - What authority does the MFC believe it has to pursue a complaint based on the content of a minister's published speech?
> - Has the MFC conducted an unbiased preliminary examination of the legitimacy and integrity of the LREDA complaint?

- What constraints do you perceive to exist on the MFC's authority to launch such an investigation based on what is clearly a meritless complaint?
- What assurances will you make that future investigators won't have conflicts of interest, as did your first choice? Do you care?
- If it is found that the LREDA complaint is without merit (as it objectively is), what measures will the MFC take to prevent something like this from happening again, to me or any other innocent minister?
- How many MFC Board members signed any of the instant, reactive, and unfounded letters against me, which clearly do violate our ethical code of conduct?

What of the hundreds of my colleagues who have very clearly violated this code of conduct by attacking me? Do you plan investigating them with the undaunted diligence driving your investigation of me?

So, as I stated in my last communication, "for now, in good conscience and for the sake of freedom of the pulpit and the freedoms of other ministers, I cannot cooperate with or legitimize this further instance of authoritarian overreach occurring within our once free and noble liberal religion."

Two days later I received another terse response: "Well received. I will review your questions, confer with the MFC, and get back to you." Although I no longer mistook the phrase "well received" as positive, I did take it to mean I would finally receive a response to my questions, which the Executive Secretary had promised to provide in the previous communication: "please let me know if you have any questions, which I will attempt to answer." Instead, on May 21, 2020, I received a response stating, "This letter is to inform you that the Ministerial Fellowship Committee has decided to convene on June 5th to consider your removal from fellowship based on your continued violation of Rule 28":

On March 30, I informed you that the Committee had voted to move forward with a full fellowship review because your unwillingness to engage with the Committee's investigation constituted an initial violation of Rule 28. You were advised to reconsider. Following the receipt of your communication on April 24, in which you stated your continued intent not to cooperate with the Committee's review process, the Committee has determined it is suspending your fellowship review and instead moving directly to a decision on your fellowship status. The extension of the Committee's process into a full fellowship review would have provided you an opportunity to appropriately share any concerns with the MFC's process and to make the case that your actions were consistent with the rules of fellowship, but in choosing not to cooperate you have forfeited your opportunity to influence the Committee's further process.

Today, a special meeting of the MFC Executive Committee met to review your continuing refusal to engage with the fellowship review process in preparation for the June 5th meeting. They noted that you have demonstrated a pattern of refusing to engage in dialogue around injury you have caused to others when informed that you are out of right relationship, of which your most recent Rule 28 violation is one example. Unfortunately, your refusal to engage has meant that conflicts which could have been addressed through mediated reparative conversation have instead been funneled through formal complaint processes, creating negative ripple effects across the broader faith community. The following examples of this refusal to engage have been noted in the Committee's process so far:

1. You refused to engage in a conversation with UUA Co-Moderator ▓▓▓▓ ▓▓▓▓ and other leaders representing LREDA and DRUUMM at General Assembly in Spokane when you initially distributed your book, causing controversy and pain for members of those communities.
2. The UU Ministers Association requested that you engage in a process of right relationship in the fall of 2019. Your refusal led to your formal censure.
3. You refused to engage in a conversation with the ▓▓▓▓▓▓ in ▓▓ role as a Consultant for Ethics and Safety after the UUA received a formal complaint of professional misconduct from LREDA, as noted above.
4. Your subsequent refusal to engage with the Committee's full fellowship review.
5. We understand from UUA staff with the Pacific Western Region that you have refused to engage in a process with your own congregational leaders who feel you have harmed them, instead fomenting divisiveness within the congregation you are covenanted to serve.

Ministry is a relational endeavor, and it is a sine qua non of fellowship as a minister in the UUA that one be willing to engage with others when there is a concern expressed that one's words or actions have caused harm, particularly to those from historically marginalized communities. We as Unitarian Universalists are called to work to repair historic and ongoing injustices to Black, Indigenous and other People of Color, to transgender and nonbinary individuals, to those who are disabled, who are poor, and others who have been marginalized, and to do so both within and beyond our faith community. We understand you have sought to focus public attention on your critiques of the UUA's approach to this work of repairing injustice, but whether you agree with a particular approach to this work is not the essential issue in the Committee's process. Rather, the refusal to engage in dialogue with others and to be accountable for your actions is the substance of the Committee's review, and the base for which it will now consider removing your fellowship.

I will be in touch as soon as the Committee makes its determination.

In this communication alone, the words "engage" and "engaged," usually prefaced by the phrases "refuse to," "refusal to," or "unwillingness to," occurs 16 times. It occurs 42 times in the MFC documents cited in just this chapter. Clearly pounding away with this justification makes the UUA, UUMA, and MFC look a lot better than admitting their un-Unitarian, illiberal, and persecutory behavior in response to a book. Yet this particular document proves their real motive by explicitly referring to the "harm you *have* caused others," a statement admitting what I knew all along, that my guilt had already been decided. This harm, the letter goes on to insinuate, resulted from my implied failure to "work to repair historic and ongoing injustices to Black, Indigenous and other People of Color, to transgender and nonbinary individuals, to those who are disabled, who are poor, and others who have been marginalized, and to do so both within and beyond our faith community." As with the UUMA censure and the LREDA complaint, the MFC interprets this standard to mean nobody can criticize their specific approach to social justice without violating their rules.

Again, I have never been invited to engage with these entities to discuss my concerns, only told to attend hostile tribunals in which my guilt had been predetermined, then further condemned, after the fact, for "refusing to engage." Simply substituting these many instances of the word "engage" with "obey" would make their claims more honest and accurate. To pretend the MFC hearings, during which I would have to fight for my credentials, conducted by those who had already demonstrated extreme prejudice, were an invitation to mutually "engage," is preposterous. Herein, I have presented a written record of the numerous times I sought responses to questions with which the MFC "refused to engage." Without any guarantee their tribunal would be fair, nor even the slightest response to my concerns, I was not about to legitimize what had shaped up to be a kangaroo court with a foregone conclusion by participating in it.

The June 5th communication further claims, "your refusal to engage has meant that conflicts which could have been addressed through mediated reparative conversation have instead been funneled through formal complaint processes, creating negative ripple effects across the broader faith community." Again, I would dispute that I was ever invited to participate in "mediated reparative conversation," appealing as they misleadingly make it sound. Indeed, the opportunity to have had an outside and impartial mediator under mutually agreed upon circumstances would have been welcomed by me. Instead, I was instructed to attend a 7:00 AM meeting to discuss "the disruption your book is causing," then "invited," in a public letter of censure calling me a white supremacist, to allow its issuers to help publicly restore me, then directed to participate in a blatantly prejudicial tribunal comprising several individuals who had already publicly determined my guilt.

I would further argue the "negative ripple effects" the MFC Executive Secretary blames me for, even before the Committee had officially met to decide the matter, were not caused by my book, but by the UUA, UUMA, and MFC's unexpected and un-Unitarian Universalist reaction to it. The controversy surrounding *The Gadfly Papers*, which helped it become an Amazon bestseller, is the result of their frantic, primitive, and unnecessary reactions to and outcries against it.

Though not surprised the MFC would continue moving ahead, I was troubled by new and specific accusations that I had "demonstrated a pattern of refusing to engage," qualified by five unsubstantiated and easily disproven claims.

- Regarding the MFC Executive Secretary's first claim that I had refused to engage with the GA Co-Moderator: I have every right to turn down a summons to a 7:00 AM meeting for the expressed purpose of satisfying somebody else's need to "discuss the disruption your book is causing at GA." I am not, nor have I ever been, an employee of the UUA. Nor, to my knowledge, had anyone from LREDA or DRUUM requested that I "engage" with them, although I had already met with five members of the GA's Right Relations Team the night before—a fact never mentioned by my accusers.
- The second assertion that the UUMA requested I engage in a process of right relations and that my refusal to do so led to my censure is utter nonsense. Just read the letter of censure (in the appendices) and look for any such criticism. Again, the first time I formally heard anything from the UUMA was in its letter of censure, which only then "invited" me into a "process of restoration," stating explicitly that the censure was because of the "psychological, spiritual, and emotional damage" my book is claimed to have caused. Nowhere does it say it was because I "refused to engage," nor does it mention any prior requests to do so.

- Regarding the third claim, that I had refused to engage with the biased investigator the MFC had assigned to the complaint, it speaks for itself. It was, in fact, the MFC that refused to engage with me about the matter by utterly ignoring my repeated and understandable concerns about the conflict of interest.
- Regarding the fourth claim, that I refused to engage with the full Fellowship Review, I declined, quite obviously, because a fair investigation had not yet occurred and the MFC would not address the matter.
- Regarding the fifth claim: I find it most troubling of all because it unfairly, cruelly, and falsely drags the good people of my congregation into the matter, repulsively and falsely using them as a means to the MFC's now obvious ends. As the previous chapter proves, the great majority in my congregation remained in support of me throughout this difficult year, despite a small number working to get rid of me. If anyone should rightfully be accused of "fomenting divisiveness" in my congregation, it is the UUA, whose staff and administration appears to have worked with our rogue Board leaders to oust me, despite the expressed wishes of most of our members. As I shall make a case for momentarily, the timing of the MFC's notice to my congregation of my disfellowship also proved convenient in this endeavor.

On May 25, 2020, Rev. Davis and I sent the following letter in response to this latest step toward the MFC's apparently predetermined decision to remove me from fellowship:

As a preface to the following communication from Rev. Eklof let me affirm that I share his concerns in regard to the manner in which you, the MFC, have handled this matter from the very beginning. Your unresponsiveness and lack of transparency in regard to our expressed concerns about the impartiality of your proceedings continues to be troubling, to say the least. Then there are your misstatements in regard to the UUMA's censure of Rev. Eklof and internal matters in his congregation. This is very alarming and only serves to validate our mistrust in your proceedings.

Given all of this and more, I urge you to pause in this process and re-consider your next steps. Rev. Eklof would be willing to engage with you once you have satisfactorily responded to his legitimate questions and given genuine assurances that this process can truly be fair and unbiased.

THE GADFLY AFFAIR

Sincerely,

Rev. Rick Davis, acting as Rev. Eklof's Good Officer

To the MFC:

On March 11, 2020, I wrote you expressing my concerns about your appointment of a person as your lead investigator for my case, who is known to have publicly maligned me and misrepresented my writings, and I asked you how I could possibly receive a fair hearing?

You responded on March 30th without addressing this crucial issue, writing, instead, "because you have been non-compliant with the initial investigation into this matter in violation of Rule 28 which requires cooperation with the Committee, they determined to recommend a full fellowship review to the full MFC at its business meeting on Sunday, March 29th."

On March 24th I replied, expressing my astonishment at your determination to plow ahead while ignoring the issue I raised about your lead investigator's obvious conflict of interest, along with several other questions and concerns about your process. Later that day, I received an email message from ▓▓▓▓▓▓ ▓▓▓▓▓▓ stating, "Well received. I will review your questions, confer with the MFC, and get back to you."

I had been eagerly awaiting your response to these concerns. So I was stunned to instead receive your May 21st letter stating you will be meeting on "June 5th to consider your removal from fellowship based on your continued violation of Rule 28," and then proceeding to erroneously claim it is I who have been unwilling to engage with you.

Such engagement must be a two-way street, not an authoritarian demand that I comply and do whatever you say without question, and no matter how unreasonable.

Again, I cannot fully participate in your investigation until you have satisfactorily addressed my concerns and demonstrated that I will truly get a fair hearing.

Instead of acknowledging in the slightest your initial missteps in launching this effort, you listed a handful of erroneous examples of my "pattern of refusal to engage." You bewilderingly state, for instance, that "The UU Ministers Association requested that you engage in a process of right relationship in the fall of 2019. Your refusal led to your formal censure."

Can you produce any evidence of this request? Because it's news to me. The (very public, widely distributed) letter of censure contains nothing in it to corroborate that claim. In fact, the letter was the first formal communication I received from the UUMA on the matter, which includes an invitation for me to "enter into a process of restoration" regarding the "harm" I have caused.

That's hardly an invitation to "engage."

I and my Good Officer have since formally written the UUMA leaders requesting they address several questions and concerns I have about this process before we can reasonably engage.

Like you, they have not been willing to do so. This one rebuttal is enough to cast doubt on your other "examples," including your blatantly false claim that I've "refused to engage" with the very investigator whose conflict of interest I've already written you twice about.

To claim I was censured because I've been refusing to engage is not just wrong, but deceitful: I was censured for writing a book of dissenting views, just as it would now appear is also the reason for your biased investigation and determination to bolt straight toward my disfellowship.

I once again invite you to honestly engage with me by reasonably addressing the concerns I previously addressed:

- Assigning a person to conduct the investigation who has publicly and, in no uncertain terms, already concluded that I was wrong to publish my book. [How can this remotely be a fair investigation?]
- Investigating a complaint that is patently specious on its face. [Why did the MFC not do a preliminary evaluation of the complaint before deciding to confront me with it?]
- Investigating a complaint based on a gratuitous interpretation of covenants to which the complainant was not a party. [The UUMA covenants are between ministers, not with non-ministerial groups such as LREDA. Why is an element of the UUA dealing with a complaint based on alleged UUMA covenants anyway?]
- Failing to address the problem that, even if having some validity, the complaint attacks my freedom of the pulpit. [The MFC did not explain to me why it felt authorized to consider a matter which would have the effect of conflicting with this core right of ministry.]

Finally, I am deeply offended by your statement:

> We understand from UUA staff with the Pacific Western Region that you have refused to engage in a process with your own congregational leaders who feel you have harmed them, instead fomenting divisiveness within the congregation you are covenanted to serve.

It's clear that the UUA/MFC and its staff have been working behind the scenes with the leadership of a small, disgruntled faction in my congregation to undermine my ministry, even though that faction does not represent the sentiments of the great majority of our members. By doing so, it is the UUA staff that has inappropriately (and quite unethically) contributed to the divisiveness within my congregation. I consider this is an unacceptable intrusion in internal congregational matters, and completely outside the organizations' charters.

How can I or anyone else in good conscience "engage" in what is so obviously a one-sided and unreasonable process?

Nonetheless I once again invite you to reconsider your course by truly opening yourselves to a mutual process of genuine curiosity and honest engagement, rather than what, until now, has seemed another attempt to drive me out of the UUA for writing a book of dissenting views.

I would very much welcome that opportunity.

Sincerely,

Rev. Dr. Todd F. Eklof

Two weeks later, on June 7, 2020, I received notice from the MFC letting me know I had been disfellowshipped, or, as I prefer to say, *excommunicated*. Unlike my other partly sardonic, partly whimsical chapter titles, the title of this chapter is in earnest. The very next day, on June 8, 2020, I received an email from the UUMA explaining:

> We have received notice from the Ministerial Fellowship Committee that you are no longer in fellowship with the UUA. Per the UUMA bylaws, UUA fellowship is a pre-requisite for UUMA membership so we will be removing you as a UUMA member effective immediately. Some of the benefits of membership that you will lose include access to a uuma.org email address, the UUMA list serves (Chat & News) and our website. We will also notify your chapter leadership and the general UUMA membership that you're no longer a member of the UUMA.
>
> If you have any questions feel free to contact me. We wish you well in the future.

EXCOMMUNICATED

With wishes for a joyous day

In UUA parlance, disfellowship is the equivalent of excommunication in other religions. Although our congregations remain autonomous, at least for now, and I am able to maintain my post so long as the members of my congregation wish me to, I am no longer welcome within the professional community of Unitarian Universalist ministers. I have been excised from such communion. As the MFC's letter of notification concludes, "Because you have been removed from fellowship a public notice will be made according to the communication policies of the MFC. While you retain your ordination, please do not present yourself in a way that would imply fellowship with the UUA."

Most of the other claims made in this letter have already been previously addressed, with one exception, which I will endeavor to explain here for the record. My letter of excommunication begins:

> You were first contacted by the Rev. ███████, Consultant for Ethics and Safety, on January 8th after the UUA received a complaint of misconduct from LREDA. The purpose of the initial investigation, as you know, was to determine whether the matter should even come before the committee. That process was stymied by your false claim to be too ill to be interviewed, followed by a general objection on principle, followed by an accusation of bias.

You will recall that it was on January 8th, 2020, that I received notification of the complaint from the MFC Executive Secretary, not from its lead investigator (Consultant for Ethics and Safety). It wasn't until February 4, 2020, that the investigator first contacted me requesting an interview:

> Rev. Eklof,
>
> I have been assigned as the investigator for the complaint filed against you by LREDA. My role is to gather relevant materials, conduct interviews and write a summary with recommendations to the Office of Ethics and Safety. I see that Rev. ███████ has outline the general parameters of the process and has made recommendations to you regarding Policy 17 c.
>
> To begin this process, I would like to schedule a conversation with you in the next couple of weeks to explore your reactions to [the] complaint.
>
> This conversation can be on zoom or we can chat on the phone. Following our conversation, it is suggested that you prepare a written response to the

complaint and add any additional materials (documents. emails etc.) that support your position.

I do understand that this is a stressful and perhaps disconcerting event for your ministry. Please know that all parties will be treated fairly and with ministerial care.

I look forward to hearing from you.

Rev. ███
UUA Consultant Investigator

At that point, I had already begun a month-long sabbatical to deal with a gastric ulcer, the first in my life, that had developed after months of extreme stress, much of which I attribute to the UUA, UUMA, and MFC's continued harassment. As the MFC letter correctly acknowledges, "Your Good Officer, the Rev. Rick Davis, responded in February that you were taking a medical leave from your congregation and would be unable to be interviewed until March. The Rev. ███ responded that ███ would look forward to speaking with you in March, and we informed LREDA that there would be a delay because of an urgent medical issue."

This much is so, but this paragraph concludes, "Later we learned that you traveled to Rick Davis' congregation in Salem OR to guest preach in February." That's right, I did! And had every right to decide how to spend my time off and to determine what was and wasn't beneficial to my particular health problem. Visiting a supportive friend and speaking before a supportive congregation, in addition to enjoying the beautiful natural surroundings in a breathtaking location for a few days, proved to be extremely healing for me. By the time my sabbatical ended, my ulcer had cleared up and has not bothered me since. I'm quite certain this would not have been the case had I instead met the biased investigator's request to undergo a stressful interview and to then concentrate my efforts on writing a response to the ludicrous complaint against me. To insinuate that the MFC has the right to determine what is and isn't the proper use of one's time off, and that I had lied about "being too ill to be interviewed," is another insulting example of its authoritarian overreach and dearth of compassion in this matter. It should be obvious that being ill doesn't necessitate being bedridden.

On March 4, 2020, I received an email from the investigator asking, "Now that you have returned from your sabbatical, is there a convenient time for us to talk about the complaint?" Having by then learned this individual had already publicly and defamatorily condemned my book, causing me to question the sincerity and legitimacy of the entire process, I responded, as previously mentioned: "For the sake of our Unitarian Universalist tradition and the future freedoms of liberal ministers, I cannot in good conscience validate such proceedings with my participation."

I won't go into the contents of the MFC's letter here because it contains the same sort of straw man arguments and red herrings that have previously been dismantled. For those interested, I have included a copy of it in the appendices of this work. Instead, I will conclude this chapter by mentioning that the notice of my excommunication was sent to me via email on Sunday evening, June 7, 2020, and had been sent to my colleagues throughout the UUA the following morning, as well as to the Board president of my church. I had intended to notify my congregation of the action myself after I returned to the office on Tuesday. As is well known in my congregation, I take Mondays off and on this particular Monday was undergoing a routine medical procedure. Upon coming out of anesthesia that afternoon, I awoke to a text from a concerned church member who had received notification from our Board of Trustees informing the entire congregation of this latest development first thing that morning, robbing me of my right to do so, not having discussed the matter with me beforehand, and opportunistically claiming it was their responsibility to let the congregation know.

My disfellowship was also a proverbial "October surprise," given it came only two days before our congregation's mail-in ballots would be sent out, providing our members the opportunity to participate in what was effectively a vote of confidence for me. Fortunately, most in my congregation, like many ministers and members throughout the UUA, were paying attention to all that had transpired up to this point and were not swayed by this apparent last-minute attempt to influence our election. As stated earlier, my ministry in Spokane was supported by an overwhelming majority in our congregation, although I am no longer welcome in the UUA or UUMA.

It should also be noted that it was only within the letter of disfellowship that the investigator's conflict of interest was finally addressed, when doing so became irrelevant, and then only briefly and unconvincingly:

> . . . you objected to the fact that the UUA Consultant had signed onto a letter at the Spokane GA objecting to the harm your book was causing to clergy of color. Notably, some 800 of our clergy signed onto such letters including virtually all of the clergy of color in our UU movement. Simply signing that letter was not grounds for recusal.

To be clear, the specific letter signed by the MFC's investigator, stating my book was the "dissemination of racism, ableism, and the affirmation of other forms of oppression, including classism and homo- and transphobia," was signed by 39 individuals, not 800. Nevertheless, the Executive Director, even while conflating it with another letter, does not explain why numerous signatures on "such letters" wasn't "grounds for recusal." According to the due process clauses of the U.S. Constitution, judges must recuse themselves if they either have financial interests in the outcome of a case, or if there is a likely possibility their decisions will be biased. Not that the MFC is required to adhere to these standards, but this unsound argument, justifying the retention of an investigator who had already demonstrated extreme prejudice, defies any reasonable understanding of what ethically ought to be involved in fair and impartial proceedings. The very fact the question was raised should have been cause enough for the MFC to find another investigator rather than waiting to say it doesn't matter in the same letter notifying me I'd been excommunicated.

ENDARKENED

Liberal institutions cease to be liberal as soon as they are attained: later on, there are no worse and no more thorough injurers of freedom than liberal institutions.
—Friedrich Nietzsche

THE WIDESPREAD SOCIAL phenomenon now manifesting within Unitarian Universalism has yet to receive its final appellation. To date it has been called political correctness (PC), safetyism, identitarianism, identity politics, cancel culture, woke, wokeness, anti-racism, postmodernism, and a few budding appellations like John McWhorter's Third Wave Anti-Racism (TWA). Since, at its core, we are considering a mindset that is the antithesis of the Enlightenment motto *Sapere Aude!* (Dare to Know), I have settled upon the term *Endarkenment*.

Upon first tossing it about, I was immediately informed by some of my liberal friends that it is no longer politically correct to use the terms "light" in ways that are positive, or "dark" in ways that are negative, a reaction that is itself demonstrative of the Endarkenment overshadowing modern times. Humanity's unconscious and primordial associations with light and darkness are archetypal components of our collective unconscious, as expressed in ancient and modern stories in many cultures. This cannot be altered simply because of the current Age of Endarkenment's linguicidal obsessions.

In George Orwell's terrifying horror novel, *1984,* the Ministry of Truth, as it is ironically named, exists for the purpose of rewriting history and controlling speech. "We're destroying words," the Ministry explains, "scores of them, hundreds of them, every day. We're cutting the language down to the bone. . . . In the end the whole notion of goodness and badness will be covered by only six words—in reality, only one word."[1] This is the first step in establishing authoritarian systems—controlling the collective mindset by controlling free speech—whether it is dominator societies restricting the use of foreign languages or colonizers forbidding the continued use of indigenous languages. "Newspeak," as Orwell calls it, "was designed not to extend but to *diminish* the range of thought, and this purpose was indirectly assisted by cutting the choice of words down to a minimum."[2] To accomplish this, the Ministry of Truth makes use of confusing *doublethink*, in which words are spun to mean their very opposite:

> WAR IS PEACE
> FREEDOM IS SLAVERY
> IGNORANCE IS STRENGTH[3]

Today we are seeing the same kind of doublethink demonstrated by the UUA and UUMA with statements I would similarly sloganize as:

> LOGIC IS RACISM
> FREE SPEECH IS OPPRESSION
> THINKING IS HARMFUL

The purpose of this isn't merely to control speech, but, ultimately, to squelch individual expression in order to control the thoughts and behaviors of others, which, again, is the very antithesis of the Enlightenment principles upon which Unitarian Universalism was founded. Without these defining principles, whether it calls itself so or not, it can no longer be considered Unitarian Universalism. This goal of utterly possessing the wills of others is also the chilling purpose of *1984's* Ministry of Truth: "We shall squeeze you empty, and then we shall fill you with ourselves."[4]

Even more indicative of what is now transpiring in Unitarian Universalism, as it is in other liberal organizations and religions, and as has been happening in Academia for more than a generation, is the dystopian novel that soon followed *1984*, Ray Bradbury's *Fahrenheit 451*. The banning and burning of books defining Bradbury's hellish future doesn't occur because of external coercion, as it does in *1984*, but because of internal cohesion. It "didn't come from the Government down," Bradbury writes. "There was no dictum, no declaration, no censorship, to start with, no! Technology, mass exploitation, and minority pressure carried the trick."[5]

When *F. 451* was published in 1954 the word "minority" was used to refer to any special interest group. "Don't step on the toes of dog-lovers, cat-lovers, doctors, lawyers, merchants, chiefs, Mormons, Baptists, Unitarians, second-generation Chinese, Swedes, Italians, Germans, Texans, Brooklynites, Irishmen, people from Oregon or Mexico."[6] Yes, Bradbury even had the foresight to include Unitarians on his list of those too sensitive to get their delicate toes stepped on. But his main premise is that as human population increases, so does the number of special interest groups, resulting in a society in which nothing can be written that doesn't offend somebody, either by stating something they disagree with or simply by excluding their particular interests. In *F. 451* this makes publishers reluctant to print anything meaningful. "The bigger your market, the less you handle controversy, remember that! All the minor minor minorities with their navels to be kept clean. Authors, full of evil thoughts, lock up your typewriters."[7]

So, in the end, the "firemen," those responsible not for putting out fires but for burning illegal stashes of books, "are rarely necessary. The public itself stopped reading of its own accord."[8] At least in Orwell's novel people have little choice but to be squeezed empty by authoritarian forces. In *F. 451* they are complicit in bringing about their own Endarkenment. In today's reality, it isn't the governments of the Free World that are doing so either, but many of their own citizens, who are forcing society to yield to the limited vocabulary sanctioned by digital hordes on social media.

Thinking for yourself, the Enlightenment motto, is forbidden in the fictional worlds of Orwell and Bradbury, and increasingly in today's real-world Endarkenment. "The word 'intellectual,' of course, became the swear word it deserved to be,"[9] Bradbury writes. Such anti-intellectualism was expressed in the very real letter signed by more than five hundred Unitarian Universalist ministers in response to *The Gadfly Papers*: "We recognize that a zealous commitment to 'logic' and 'reason' over all other forms of knowing is one of the foundational stones of White Supremacy Culture," and, "predictable 'freedom of speech' arguments are commonly weaponized to perpetuate oppression and inflict further harm."

Today, due to social media, there is no need to go to court, to present evidence, or to allow anyone a defense. Just compose a quick, thoughtless, unfounded statement, press "enter," and condemn or cancel anyone you wish. To hell with fairness and facts! It is chilling and it is why so many of us are afraid to confront the situation. For it is difficult to survive being condemned as racist, homophobic, transphobic, ableist, classist, etc., etc., when such accusations, proven or not, are only a prospective or current employer's Google search away. Speaking one's own authentic mind in such dark times takes fortitude, a strength those understandably intimidated by digital mobs do not have. Rather, in seeking to remain inconspicuous, as in the world of *F. 451*, in which only meaningless comic books and pornography have survived the literary purge, they fail to achieve what social psychologist Erich Fromm considers the whole purpose of life, "the duty to become oneself."[10] Or, as Kant put it, "This immaturity is self-imposed when its cause lies not in lack of understanding, but in lack of resolve and courage to use it without guidance from another."[11] No "dictum, no declaration, no censorship," is necessary. "Technology, mass exploitation, and minority pressure carried the trick."

When confronted with concerns about the direction Unitarian Universalism is heading, especially regarding its decline in membership, some supporting this dark turn have made statements like, "If people aren't leaving, we're not doing our job," or, "Maybe UUism has to disappear in order to make room for what's next." Because these are anecdotal statements, we have no means of knowing how many may share these views but, in light of all I have witnessed since distributing *The Gadfly Papers*, I cannot but think such views are widespread.

Certainly, every religion, as well as any belief system, has its flaws and inadequacies, can always be improved upon, and needs to evolve. As Master Morehei Ueshiba, the founder of Aikido, said, "Life is growth. If we stop growing, technically and spiritually, we are as good as dead."[12] I believe those seeking to "transform" Unitarian Universalism remain faithful to this principle. If only they also remained faithful to the religion that they have been entrusted to serve! Authoritarian movements are always utopian in their endeavors, and utopias are always to be established upon the abolition and demolition of all that has come before. If the world is imperfect, they erroneously infer that by ending it entirely they can purge its imperfections. Only then, like the Babylonian god Marduk after slaying the sea monster Tiamat, can they refashion their new, perfect, ideal world from the remains of its dead corpse—establishing order out of chaos.

As Polish philosopher and Statesman, Ryszard Legutko explains in *The Demon in Democracy*, his 2016 book about totalitarian tendencies in free societies, highlighting the similarities between liberal democracies and the communist society he grew up in: "Both are utopian and look forward to 'an end of history' where their systems will prevail as a permanent status quo[13]. . . . [E]verything—in both communism and liberal democracy—should be modern: thinking, family, school, literature, and philosophy. If a thing, a quality, an attitude, an idea is not modern, it should be modernized or will end up in the dustbin of history."[14]

The wish to make the world a better place is admirable, if not categorically imperative. As with life, a society that doesn't grow and evolve is as good as dead. Yet no society will ever be perfect and would probably be miserably boring if it were. What would life be without its challenges, without the possibility of becoming, without the freedom to make mistakes one can learn from? The word *utopia* means, "no place," yet I believe its attainment is the misguided motivation underlying the recent usurpation and evisceration of what was once the world's most liberal religion.

I discuss what I believe to be the origins of its slow demise in *The Gadfly Papers*, which I trace back to the identity crisis that emerged immediately after the formation of the Unitarian Universalist Association in 1961. The trend has been worsening ever since, and now, with no true identity of its own, the Association has come to worship the identities of others, turning this idolatrous totem into a taboo that is strictly guarded and that no one may disrupt. I also believe it is the most recent attempt to resolve this identity crisis, by building a completely new identity out of Unitarian Universalism's remains, that explains the troubling authoritarian turn the UUA and UUMA are now demonstrating.

I'm told the 20th century philosopher Stephen Toulmin used to tell his students, "To earn the right to criticize someone you must first understand their argument well enough to present it in a way they would accept as informed and fair." It is in this spirit I will now attempt to explain the points made in an essay entitled, "From iChurch to Beloved Community: Ecclesiology and Justice," presented by Rev. Fredric Muir at an annual meeting of the UUMA just prior to the 2012 General Assembly in Phoenix, Arizona, which I believe has become the blueprint for Unitarian Universalism's deconstruction.

Rev. Muir's essay, about the future of Unitarian Universalism begins by pointing out its stagnant membership numbers: "In spite of being a justice-seeking faith, in spite of the ministries to which we are committed, in spite of the marketing we have done," he says, "we have not grown." Rather, our religion is at a "tipping point" and if we don't recognize it and respond accordingly, we will not be a "religion of the future."

Additionally, Rev. Muir says, there is a confluence of other factors that have led to a "perfect storm" that we have failed to recognize. Chief among them is the U.S. Census Bureau's prediction that by 2042 "members of racial and ethnic minorities will make up a majority of the country's population." From this he concludes that if Unitarian Universalism continues to maintain its "North Atlantic look—as reflected in our demographics, theology, and epistemology—[it] will grow more cut off from the U.S. population, unless we start reflecting our society's true diversity." He further points out that, according to much research, those indicating they have no religion, the "Nones," are the fastest growing religious identity group in the U.S. From this, he further concludes that if Unitarian Universalism is to grow, it will only be by better appealing to these growing demographics. "Ministry to and with 'minorities' (that is, those who make little-to-no claim on a North Atlantic heritage), along with a ministry to the 'Nones' could be a ministry of growth or justice making."

But it isn't only our "North Atlantic like" look we must be willing to alter to make this happen, but also our faulty North Atlantic theology and epistemology. "Fundamental to our future," he says, "is recognizing that our way of faith, from its ministry to its members, has been supported and nurtured by a trinity of errors, leading not only to ineffectiveness but to an inability to share our liberating message":

- First, we are being held back and stymied by a persistent, pervasive, disturbing, and disruptive commitment to individualism that misguides our ability to engage the changing times;
- Second, we cling to a Unitarian Universalist exceptionalism that is often insulting to others and undermines our good news;
- Third, we refuse to acknowledge and treat our allergy to authority and power, though all the symptoms compromise a healthy future.

"These three organizing and corrupting narratives have shaped our story," a story he recommends we transform before we can successfully move "From iChurch to Beloved Community":

> In this process, we will create something that has eluded Unitarian Universalism: a doctrine of church, an ecclesiology that is grounded in congregational justice making, a doctrine of church that will guide and sustain us as we become the religion we (and others) know we can be.

In discussing the first of these errors, *individualism*, Rev. Muir begins by explaining how transformative and central Emersonian Transcendentalism had been in his own life and ministry but that he eventually recognized as the origin of a faulty nationwide story. "That story," he says, "is about American uniqueness and individualism and has been expressed in a myriad of ways." After further discussing his creative use of the term "iChurch" by use of cultural phenomena like Apple's iPhone and iconic nonconformists like Jack Kerouac, Rev. Muir makes the case that "Individualism not only shaped American culture writ large but shaped Unitarian Universalism: We comprise the church of Emersonian individualism; we are the iChurch."

Rev. Muir distinguishes between "individuality" and "individualism" in his critique of the latter, explaining, "I have read enough of Emerson to feel certain that he celebrated the gifts of individuality, the beauty of nature's differences and diversity, of which humans are a part," but "When used as an expression of individualism rather than an expression of the joy and celebration of individuality, the Principles come dangerously close to sounding like an ideology or creed turned theology and spirituality." Yet this is precisely what he believes has transpired in Unitarian Universalism, which "took the blessing and joy of individuality and made it an ideology, made it a theology, and did a very bad job of making it polity," resulting in what he calls a group of "atomic and unrelated individuals." As such, he says, "There is little to nothing about the ideology and theology of individualism that encourages people to work and live together, to create and support institutions that serve common aspirations and beloved principles."

His proposed solution to individualism is "covenant," which he considers a "promise" between Unitarian Universalists guaranteeing "mutual trust and support." This is so, he believes, because "We cannot do both covenant and individualism," the two cannot coexist. He considers *individualism* the worst of the three errors because the other two—"exceptionalism" and our "allergy to authority and power"—are but its outgrowths.

Rev. Muir contextualizes exceptionalism as the belief that "Unitarian Universalism is a faith shaped by 'perceptions, ideas, intuitions, and ambitions which posits, among other things, that [our way of religion] is uniquely virtuous, uniquely powerful, uniquely destined to accomplish great things, and thus uniquely authorized to act in ways to which [Unitarian Universalists] would object if done by other [ways of faith].'" He further suggests that outsiders often experience this pervasive attitude as off-putting and insulting:

> Whether as a source of pride, personal and community truth, embellishment, anger, clarification, or, strangely enough, welcoming—we hear the inflection of Unitarian Universalist exceptionalism from the pulpit, from newcomer's classes, from Sunday greeters, from those who are earnestly trying to explain our way of religion to the uninformed. As unique as our experience with Unitarian Universalism may be, it is not the only way. We must stay conscious of how we explain, defend, or share lest we come across as elitist, insulting, degrading, isolating, even humiliating of others.

Going on to discuss what he means by "our allergy to authority and power," Rev. Muir acknowledges that there are "many reasons to be suspicious of hierarchical structures," especially for the many who found Unitarian Universalism after leaving other "faith communities where no room was made for different views or disagreements." After admitting having once been lured into Emersonian nonconformity himself, by "conflating the narrow path of individualism with the promise of institutional health," he now believes "Unitarian Universalism's allergy and misuse of power and authority is a factor in our inability or unwillingness to welcome and listen to a diversity of interests and passions." What he calls the "antidote" for this allergy is, again, a covenant "promising our mutual trust and support." In congregations where such a promise has occurred, he says, "there is a clear and deep understanding that addresses the potential of abuse and misuse of authority and power, those ministries are among our most vibrant, growing, and electric."

From here, Rev. Muir imagines what might happen if this antidote were to become widespread: "If individualism led us to the iChurch, then covenant can shape the beloved community." This phrase was popularized by Dr. Martin Luther King, Jr., who said, "I understand the term Beloved Community to mean an inclusive, interrelated society based on love, compassion, responsibility, shared power, and a respect for all people, places, and things—a society that radically transforms individuals and restructures institutions." Such institutional change will begin, Rev. Muir posits, by creating a new story about who "we will be, who we are becoming," that speaks "not only [of] our historical commitment to social justice outreach but with congregational justice inreach." Overemphasizing outreach can be used as an excuse to avoid doing the hard work of dismantling the trinity of errors, he says: "And how convenient to want to reform the world because the work of shaping and modeling our congregations as beloved communities, not as the iChurch, means addressing the challenges of individualism, exceptionalism, and authority."

This does not mean completely abandoning what he calls "our historical journey of justice making in the world," but narrowing it down to multiculturalism and anti-racism, environmental justice, sexual and family values, and right relationships, which he says should become the "four pillars of our justice-seeking and justice-making ecclesiology [and] the foundation on which every Unitarian Universalist beloved community is built." He then concludes by proposing Unitarian Universalism must become "religious and spiritual." Although he doesn't go into great detail about what this means, he does indicate it refers to something that was lost when Unitarians took a "humanistic, arguably post-Christian turn in the late nineteenth century that arrested its theological creativity." Admitting the reform he has outlined won't be easy, he concludes by emphasizing it cannot happen without dedicated

Unitarian Universalist ministers who are willing to implement it in their own congregations:

> An ecclesiology of beloved community that is built on the promise of mutual trust and support; Unitarian Universalism's letting go of iChurch; addressing the obstacles of exceptionalism, power, and authority; becoming congregations that are religious and spiritual—these will not happen without the bold and prophetic leadership of you, dear colleagues, you who our congregations and programs have called and hired to preach, teach, model, and lead the way.

Having now done my best to fairly explain his positions, I will add that I don't recall ever having had the privilege of meeting Rev. Muir, although I admire his courage in presenting such a challenging view of Unitarian Universalism to his colleagues, an activity that is increasingly frowned upon these days. I also appreciate his creative attempt to help resolve Unitarian Universalism's ongoing identity crisis. I would also point out that I agree with his assertion that exceptionalism and antiauthoritarianism are outgrowths of individualism, although I don't consider this a problem. A society that does not believe in individual freedom and expression, which, as a belief, is an *ism*—an individual-*ism*—will allow few to stand out as exceptional and must suppress any signs of anti-authoritarian behavior and dissent.

Beyond this, there is much I disagree with, including a few logical fallacies, *non sequiturs*, and unsupported conclusions there is no need to delve into here. I will focus, rather, on my most pertinent areas of disagreement. Firstly, I disagree that the growth of its membership should be the most crucial concern of the Unitarian Universalist Association, especially if growing requires us to fundamentally change who we are. I have no issue with it becoming less "North Atlantic" looking, as Rev. Muir puts it, which I believe it has been achieving quite organically on its own. As I mention in *The Gadfly Papers*, some of the same surveys he cites about religion in America also inform us that the number of white members in the UUA decreased from 90 percent to 75 percent between 1990 and 2008, as the number of nonwhite members increased from 11 to 25 percent. That's a 14 percent increase compared to an 11 percent increase in the U.S. overall.[15] Today, according a 2015 Pew Research study, membership among "Unitarians and other liberal faiths" is now 78 percent white, which is on par with the makeup of the U.S. population in general.[16]

But the suggestion that we must also change our theology and epistemology should not go unaddressed because it would require Unitarian

Universalism to become something fundamentally different than it is. It would require it to become another religion altogether. Theologically, Unitarian Universalism is a nontheistic religion, like Buddhism, Hinduism, and Religious Humanism. This doesn't mean some of its individual members don't believe in a deity. Many of them do. Perhaps a majority of them do. It means, rather, that we are not bound together by a particular and common belief about God. We are not defined by one theological idea. Epistemologically, we are Enlightenment thinkers, meaning that the freedom to think and speak for ourselves is our categorical imperative, as it was for Kant. If this were to change, there would be little reason for many of us to remain Unitarian Universalists, which, it appears, would suit some others well.

This would be especially true if, as Rev. Muir suggests, we become whatever we must to entice the "Nones" to join our ranks. According to numerous independent religious identity surveys, those indicating they have no religious affiliation are not only the fastest growing group in America but now represent its fourth largest religious identity group, representing over 33-million people. Conversely, a decline of membership is found among all religions in the U.S., not just Unitarian Universalism, including those that may already have the alternate "religious and spiritual" theologies and epistemologies Rev. Muir is advocating our liberal religion should take on. He is right in pointing out the majority of the Nones describe themselves as "spiritual but not religious," the meaning of which is not defined in the surveys. What we do know about the SBNRs, as they are called, is that the majority of them, including 65 percent of those between ages 18 and 30, consider themselves Christian, although they rarely if ever go to church.[17] In practice, what they mean by "spiritual but not religious" is "Christian but not churchgoing."

This would imply that in order to accommodate the Nones, Unitarian Universalism must first become more Christian in its theology and epistemology, then find a way to surmount their reluctance to attend church. It should also be noted, according to the 2012 Pew Research Rev. Muir's essay draws some of its inferences from, that 13 million of the 33 million Nones, representing 6 percent of the U.S. population, describe themselves as atheists and agnostics.[18] These surveys are already several years old, but given the trends, the numbers are likely to have increased considerably. So, even if Unitarian Universalism was to become theologically Christian to accommodate most Nones, which most other shrinking religions in the U.S. already are, repelling a huge portion of the atheists and agnostics among them in the process, there remains no sound reason to expect that doing so would be enough to entice any of the Nones to begin coming to our more-of-the-same churches.

In addition to disagreeing with what I consider this illogical growth strategy, and the implication our growth and future should supersede all else, even if it means abandoning those principles that make us who we are, our nontheistic theology and Enlightenment epistemology—which, by the way, are not exclusively "North Atlantic"—I fundamentally disagree that individualism, exceptionalism, and our aversion to authority and power are Unitarian Universalism's errors. Rather, I consider them its Trinity of Truths. Individualism, especially, is an outgrowth of our Enlightenment heritage, though it is not what Muir perceives as a group of "atomic and unrelated individuals" who have no reason to cooperate with each other.

The individualism I'm talking about refers to groups or communities bound by a shared commitment to secure and support the freedoms and flourishing of all individuals, reflecting the kind of universalizing faith that developmental psychologist James Fowler considers the highest stage of faith development: "Their community is universal in extent. Particularities are cherished because they are vessels of the universal."[19] This commitment to the sacredness of each individual as an expression of the Universal is the common belief—the *ism*—that has traditionally held Unitarian, and later, Unitarian Universalist communities together. In my experience, it has fostered profoundly meaningful relationships and cooperation between its members, not resulted in those that Rev. Muir claims have no reason to "work and live together" or "to create and support institutions that serve common aspirations and beloved principles." Nor, as far as I'm concerned, do we need to become "religious and spiritual." We already are, and deeply so. Our historic commitment to the freedom and flourishing of every individual is our religion and its spirituality.

Regarding his claims about Unitarian Universalist exceptionalism: my thirty years of experience as both a Unitarian Universalist and a Unitarian Universalist minister has seemingly been quite different than Muir's. Having visited and worked with many congregations over the years, I have not witnessed any of their members who have claimed ours is "the only way." On the contrary, I would describe this as the very opposite of my experience and the antithesis of our liberal religion. Yet I would also argue that our religion is unique in this way and, thus, demonstrates many exceptions to what is commonly thought to be indicative of religion in general. At least until now, it has been nondogmatic, noncreedal, nontheistic, and open to the influence of reason, science, dissent, and the wisdom of other faith traditions, which I consider exceptional.

Believing our way is exceptional is different from considering it the only way. So why shouldn't its ministers preach about its exceptions, or its members not speak of them when explaining their unique religion to others? If any religion were not considered exceptional, even in small ways, why would anyone choose to be part of it instead of another? In practice, however, as I argue in *The Gadfly Papers*, the opposite is more often true. Most Unitarian Universalists cannot easily explain their religion due to its decades-long identity crisis (which did not exist prior to the 1961 merger of these two faiths):

> Our common quest for the elusive "elevator speech" to explain what Unitarian Universalism means is but one symptom of our own organization's identity crisis. After more than five decades since the merger, many Unitarian Universalists still don't know how to adequately describe their religion to themselves, let alone to others. Some find it with so little meaning of its own that they feel compelled to add other traditions to the mix, describing themselves as Buddhist UUs, Christian UUs, Pagan UUs, Humanist UUs, etc., etc.[20]

Given that our disparate experiences are mostly anecdotal, I must leave it to our readers to determine for themselves which perspective they believe rings truer, mine or Rev. Muir's. However, as I also note in *The Gadfly Papers*, a 2005 UUA Commission on Appraisal report entitled "Engaging our Theological Diversity," sought to help resolve the identity question by asking, "What holds us together?" After receiving many widely differing responses, the report concludes, "Despite consensus within the church that the liberal message of Unitarian Universalism is important in this troubled world, we find it difficult to articulate that message clearly."[21] This data would indicate that few Unitarian Universalists feel secure enough to describe their religion to others with the insulting degree of certitude Muir describes.

I would also make the case that a purely negative understanding of exceptionalism is rooted in an even more pervasive misunderstanding of *equality*. As Erich Fromm once complained, "Equality today means 'sameness,' rather than oneness."[22] This subtle, though prevalent, misunderstanding has led to all manner of oppression and injustice because of its misguided belief that fairness means everyone must be treated exactly the same, have the same, earn the same, do the same, and, above all, think and say the same as everyone else. In such a society, anyone who stands out, who is an exception to the rules, becomes suspect and, often, is made to disappear in one way or another.

During my infamous February 2020 sabbatical, Rev. Davis and I were walking about Silver Falls State Park in aptly named Sublimity, Oregon, when, by chance, we passed a young boy shaking his fist while standing over a smaller boy. "You're making me mad," he said. "There are no losers. Everyone is a winner." As strange as it was to see such a young child angrily dominating another in the name of fairness, I immediately recognized it as a familiar ethic in today's society. In the name of equality and justice, everybody is a winner, no exceptions. I wondered if he was one of the many unfortunate kids these days who has engaged in contests and competitions after which everyone gets a prize. I even wondered if he may have learned his fist-shaking ethic of no exceptions in a Unitarian Universalist Religious Education program.

The same confusion also applies to some understandings of *equity*. Its meaning has been depicted by a familiar image of a group of children standing atop different sized boxes so that they are all the same height when looking over a tall fence. It is an appropriate image for depicting what must occur for every individual to have fair access to society's benefits and opportunities (although true equity might be better achieved by removing the fence that's in everyone's way). When it comes to providing basic human needs, like healthy food, clean water, fresh air, adequate housing, affordable healthcare, quality education, meaningful employment, and safe neighborhoods, as well as essential human rights like freedom of speech, ease of voting, fair taxation, and equal protections and treatment under the law, then everyone should be treated the same. Justice, that is, should be blind.

But take the same uneven vertical placement created by those different sized boxes, lay it horizontal on the ground, and make it the starting line for a hundred-meter dash. What would be the point of the race if its starting line, or finish line for that matter, were adjusted to make certain every runner finishes at once? So that "there are no losers. Everyone is a winner?" Why play any sort of game, a professional game of basketball or a friendly game of Scrabble, if the point isn't to do our best to win? And what would any enterprise or effort be without those who make exceptional contributions and accomplishments? What would any society, discipline, or vocation be without its innovators, outliers, rebels, misfits, and superstars who stand out as exceptional? What would our world be if cleansed of its Einsteins, Mozarts, and Mother Teresas? Or without the ability to stand upon the shoulders of giants? Or without those who take giant leaps for the rest of us? Life would be meaningless if, as individuals, we were not allowed to excel and stand out among others for our excellence, nor recognized for our exceptional achievements, nor allowed the pleasure and pride of an occasional win.

None of this is to argue that Unitarian Universalism, although exceptional in many ways, is the best and only way. But those of us who choose it, after considering and experiencing other options, have found it the best way for ourselves and may very well think it the best there is. Should we settle for what we consider the second, or third, or fourth, or even the last best option? Are all religions, and by extension, all beliefs and ideas, equally sound? Of course not. There are reasons we choose one religion over all others. Viewing one's religion as the best doesn't necessarily mean one wishes to force it upon others, nor result in the belittling of those who have chosen a different path. The quality of embracing and supporting those of other faiths is itself an example of Unitarian Universalism's exceptional approach to religion, and always has been.

What Rev. Muir calls "our allergy to authority and power" is another such quality. Unitarian Universalists are often, by nature, suspicious of those in authority, including those in positions of power within their own congregations. This attitude can create quite a few headaches for ministers, staff, and Board members entrusted with the responsibilities of carrying out its ordinary business and operations. But such struggle is indicative of the messiness of any democracy, does not have to be overwhelming, destructive, or discouraging, and is worth navigating through because it is better than any alternative. I personally don't wish to be part of any organization in which the masses obey those in authority without question, nor will I be, which is why I'm pushing back against what I perceive to be the authoritarian takeover of the UUA and UUMA.

Sigmund Freud once said, "Civilization has to be defended against the individual, and its regulations, institutions and commands are directed to that task."[23] This, I would suggest, is true of any group or community seeking to suppress individual expression and exceptionalism in order to maintain control of its messaging and mindset. Rev. Muir suggests this can be accomplished by eliminating individualism, exceptionalism, and anti-authoritarianism at once by initiating overarching covenantal requirements.

I know first-hand, however, that this solution is currently being used as a tool for preventing individual expression within the UUA and UUMA, having been repeatedly accused of being "out of covenant" following the distribution of *The Gadfly Papers*. "Covenant" is now but a euphemism for suppressing free thought, free speech, and dissent in our religion, which is the real violation of our promise to each other, a violation of the epistemological basis of our common values and shared principles. For it is our commitment to individual freedom and flourishing that holds us together, bonds our communities, and gives us the joy of being together with plenty of reason to work, cooperate, and struggle together. The attempt to silence me and others in our faith by tenuously claiming we have "violated covenant" cannot result in the more inclusive religion Rev. Muir promises his new Doctrine of Church and its new ecclesiology will deliver. It can only transform this once curious and friendly liberal religion into the same disparaging, depressing, dogmatic kind of religion many of its members once left.

So why have I considered it important enough to draw unnecessary attention to an essay I disagree with and that most are unlikely to have otherwise ever heard of? First, we should not be afraid of people being exposed to ideas we disagree with. Just because I disagree with Rev. Muir doesn't mean I think ill of him, nor that I don't believe he's begun a valuable dialogue for all of us, nor that I think he has in any way harmed me or anyone else. On the contrary, I am grateful for the provocative essay he's gifted us with because it has helped me better clarify my own thinking about our religion and to more clearly grasp what's currently happening to Unitarian Universalism. Ideas should not be feared or stifled but discussed with courage and gratitude. Although, if you have gratitude, you don't really need the courage.

Contrast this attitude with the response to *The Gadfly Papers* at the 2019 UUA General Assembly: After I was banned, a box of books I'd left at our church booth in the exhibit hall was confiscated, and some of our members were verbally assaulted by other Unitarian Universalists for placing them on our table. One UU minister in attendance later bragged to his congregation that he took an entire stack of them, then discarded them in the nearest trash can. If this is what the new covenantal promise to each other is to look like, I want no part of it. Like biblical Noah, who so fears and hates the old world that he bases his utopian hopes upon its complete destruction, I believe characterizing Unitarian Universalism's defining strengths as a trinity of errors is a misguided effort to do the same. Yet, be forewarned, as with Noah, any who are not fully on board with this new vision for Unitarian Universalism may find themselves left out in the rain.

Those who are on board with the destruction of our religion, the soft book burners, the confiscators of ideas, the assaulters of reason, should heed the story of Noah and his ark. For after the world is utterly destroyed and its flood waters finally recede, Noah is overwhelmed by his vision for the promising new world, purified of all its former evils and imperfections. "I have set my rainbow in the clouds," Yahweh assures him, "and it will be the sign of the covenant between me and the earth. . . . Never again will the waters become a flood to destroy all life."[24]

Interesting that this word "covenant" appears in what becomes a cautionary tale of utopian disappointment. For, in the very next verse, the one immediately following the rainbow promise, we find Noah drunk, passed out, and bare-naked inside his tent—a dramatic cut from an idyllic scene to its complete opposite. After his son Shem attempts to get his brothers to deal with their father's alcoholism, they instead try to cover it up. Shem gets kicked out of the family, and his descendants are condemned to be enslaved and exploited for the rest of eternity. So much for utopia, especially one that has been constructed on hate and fear and the ruin of other lives.

The second reason it is important to spend a good amount of time considering the contents of Rev. Muir's 2012 essay is because it has had a profound influence on what has since transpired in the Unitarian Universalist Association. In October of 2015, for example, the UUA Board of Trustees approved the formation of a Task Force on Re-Covenanting (also called "Renew the Covenant Task Force" and "Task Force on Re-Imagining Covenant"), charging it with "imagining a future for our association in which congregations were not merely members of an organization, but related to the whole dynamically and organically: through covenants, that could be renewed periodically."[25] The Task Force's first report a few months later (January 2016) calls the traditional membership model, in which congregations remain autonomous, an "atomistic model [that] reifies the independence rather than interdependence of the congregations." It later recommends "that eventually, the covenanting relationship replace membership." This is so even though, as the report itself acknowledges, the current bylaws state, "The primary purpose of the Association is to serve the needs of its member congregations,"[26] which it would have to convince General Assembly delegates to dramatically alter in order to officially carry out changes that already appear underway.

A few months later, at the 2016 General Assembly in Columbus, Ohio, the UUA Moderator at the time began his annual report by holding up and recommending everyone read a book edited by Rev. Muir entitled, *Turning Point: Essays on a New Unitarian Universalism* (2016), while discussing proposed changes to the Association's governance structure. "Muir challenges us to correct and acknowledge our trinity of errors," the Moderator said. "He writes . . . 'Fundamental to our future is recognizing our way of faith, from its leadership, to its Sunday service, to justice-making partnerships, have been supported and nurtured by this trinity of errors leading not only to ineffectiveness but also to an inability to share our liberating message.'"

After then describing Rev. Muir's trinity of errors in detail and going on to say more about his ideas for changing Unitarian Universalism, including the need for "imagination," the Moderator notes that "District leaders are imagining other ways of shaping governance. Three districts in the Midwest consolidated into one region two years ago. And eight districts in the south and central Northeast have voted to dissolve and defer governance to the UUA." He then mentions the Task Force on Re-Covenanting and his vision that "rather than signing the book, people were welcomed into covenant that would be renewed periodically. Imagine if congregations and communities entered into, were welcomed into mutual covenant with the larger Association that would be renewed periodically."

Later, in October of 2017, the Task Force on Re-Convening reported, "We have also addressed ways in which congregations and covenanted communities enter into covenant with the UUA, and with each other. We offered the example of periodic, affirmative renewal of covenant rather than our current system of membership." In its recommendations to the UUA Board of Trustees later that same year (April 2017), it had similarly stated, "The Task Force was charged with changing the culture of the UUA from one of a member services administration to one of mutual covenanting," going on to explicitly say, "The Task Force will bring to the 2018 General Assembly recommended bylaw changes that would require member congregations and covenanting communities to renew their connection to the UUA biennially, with a vote of intention to join, and a statement of how they understand their community to be fulfilling Unitarian Universalist purpose."

To my knowledge, this recommendation has yet to be fulfilled, but such talk continues at the highest administrative level. In a 2019 *UU World* article entitled "The Power of We," the Association's President also cited Muir's trinity of errors—individualism, exceptionalism, and our allergy to authority—and repeated his call to move from "iChurch to beloved community," along with his claim that covenant is the "antidote to individualism."[27] The following October, a Pacific Northwest UU Regional newsletter also contained an article using Muir's language by promoting what it called our congregational shift from "I" to "We." It would now appear the shift to a "covenantal model" is stealthily occurring without what would likely be a controversial attempt to change the Association's bylaws.

For many, such euphemisms may sound benign enough to go unnoticed: *we, beloved community, promise, mutual covenant, renewed periodically, imagine such a future.* I need not imagine such a future because I have already witnessed where it is leading, and it is not the kind of future I want for our religion. It has, in fact, already resulted in increased authority and power being "deferred to the UUA," in which dissent and disagreement are unforgivingly and immediately shut down in the name of "covenant," and in a "beloved community" in which "we" are all made afraid to talk to each other. It has led to a hostile environment in which the opposite of Rev. Muir's vision has occurred, in which many now do act as if their way is the only way and are willing to immediately condemn and make an example of anyone considered an ideological threat to their extremist views.

Not to be overlooked is the recommendation that the official covenant, whatever it becomes, should be "periodically renewed," with a biannual vote from each congregation, along with a statement explaining how they are fulfilling "the Unitarian Universalist purpose." So while we are imagining, let's imagine what might happen if a congregation doesn't fully agree with the renewed "covenant" it's being asked to accept. Or what might happen if its explanation of how it's cooperating isn't good enough. Or if it continues to support a minister who has been officially excommunicated after being branded racist, homophobic, transphobic, ableist, and classist. What happens after the UUA's transformation from a member service organization into a covenantal institution, which has successfully consolidated its power for the purpose of assuring better "cooperation and accountability," is complete?

---

[1] Orwell, George, *1984*, Signet Classics, Harcourt Inc., Penguin Group (USA), 1949, p. 51.
[2] Ibid., p. 300.
[3] Ibid., p. 4.
[4] Ibid., p. 256.
[5] Bradbury, Ray, *Fahrenheit 451*, Simon and Schuster Paperbacks, New York, NY, 1951, 2013, p. 55.
[6] Ibid., p. 54.
[7] Ibid., p. 54.
[8] Ibid., p. 83
[9] Ibid., p. 55.

[10] Fromm, Erich, *Man for Himself*, Henry Holt & Company, New York, NY, 1947, p. 20.
[11] Kant, ibid.
[12] Ueshiba, Morehei, *The Art of Peace,* Stevens, John, Trans & Ed., Shambala Press, Boston, MA, 2002, p. 23
[13] Legutko, Ryszard. The Demon in Democracy: Totalitarian Temptations in Free Societies (p. viii). Encounter Books. Kindle Edition.
[14] Ibid.
[15] Eklof, ibid., p. 98.
[16] Ibid.
[17] Grossman, Cathy Lynn, "72% of Millennials More Religious than Spiritual," *USA Today*, April 27, 2010
[18] Pew Research Center, "Nones" on the Rise: One-in-Five Adults Have No Religious Affiliation," The Pew Forum on Religion and Public Life, Released October 9, 2012.
[19] Munsey, Brenda, ed., *Moral Development, Moral Education, and Kohlberg*, Religious Education Press, Birmingham, AL, 1980, p. 149.
[20] Eklof, ibid., p. 69.
[21] Ibid., p. 70f.
[22] Fromm, Erich, *The Art of Loving*, A Bantam Book, Harper & Row, New York, NY, 1956, 1963, p. 12.
[23] Freud, Sigmund, *The Future of an Illusion*, W.W. Norton & Company, New York, NY, 1961, 1989, p. 7.
[24] *Genesis* 9:13-15
[25] Report of the UUA Task Force on Covenanting to the UUA Board, January 2016
[26] UUA Bylaws, Section C.2.2.
[27] Frederick-Gray, Susan, "The Power of We," *UU World*, Spring 2019.

AFTER WORDS

If liberty means anything at all, it means the right to tell people what they do not want to hear.

—George Orwell

AUTHORITARIANISM HAS within it a form of Puritanism that enforces rigid rules and rituals, which are often arbitrary and do nothing to help resolve real-world problems. The Pharisees, as depicted in the Christian gospels, are a good example. As theologian William Herzog explains, they believed, "For the body of Israel to replicate that level of purity or holiness in their everyday lives, all of Israel must achieve the kind of purity embodied in the temple and modeled by priests."[1] Effectively, they were a dietary cult obsessed with the idea that *cleanliness is next to Godliness*. "The Pharisees were a table companionship sect that attempted to transform every meal into a ritual of purity equal to that of the priests consuming a meal in the temple."[2] Nothing was as important in their lives as obeying inconsequential rules around proper handwashing, eating habits, and appropriate tablemates. This is why they criticized Jesus for having meals with those they considered ritually unclean: "Why do you eat and drink with tax collectors and sinners?"[3] Compassion and inclusion were eclipsed by their unforgiving purity code.

In Christendom, puritanical spirituality has been ideological, not dietary, meaning it has been embodied in rigid dogmas and doctrines for the purpose of controlling the speech and thinking of others with the larger intention of controlling the collective mindset shared by all. Linguistic purity was its motivation for the persecution and punishment of heretics and nonbelievers, the exploitation of the *Pagani* (country folk), the Crusades against Muslims, and the Catholic Inquisitions. Nobody anywhere could be permitted to hold or express unsanctioned ideas.

As noted in my introduction, after Christianity became the official Roman religion in the 4th century CE, this hypersensitive intolerance of different beliefs led to the historic Dark Ages, during which any sort of expression that did not reflect orthodox Christianity was suppressed. Everything—language, ideas, literature, art, music, science, philosophy—had to be expressed in strictly orthodox terms. Today, the movement that began approximately forty years ago in academia, once a bulwark of Enlightenment principles, has resulted in expressions of self-righteous, punitive, ideological intolerance akin to that of the Medieval Church. Armed now with the full force of social media to enact instantaneous mob justice against anyone they wish, today's linguistic puritans prove no less intolerant. They leave their pitchforks and torches at home, along with themselves, while kneeling before their omnipotent devices to do the holy work of exacting vengeance in the name of an angry god. They disinvite and dis-platform their god's wicked enemies with the lazy touch of a screen, or get them fired from their jobs, then blacklisted so they may never work again, all with no more shame, sanity, or afterthought than those who once cried "witch" in Salem or "communist" during the Red Scare. Only now they shout "racist," "homophobe," "transphobe," "ableist," and have substituted "harm" for "heresy" in their mad crusade to purify unclean lips.

As during the first Endarkenment, when everything had to be expressed through orthodox Christian dogma, today individuals and institutions are increasingly pressured to uphold this new orthodoxy in all they do and speak. An increasing number of college science professors are being reprimanded or fired for talking about the reality of biological sex, even as professors in general must issue trigger warnings before uttering anything that might possibly offend the delicate sensitivities of their fragile students, who are becoming even more fragile in the process. As of 2020, the Academy of Motion Picture Arts and Sciences now has quotas based on race, sexuality, disability, and gender regarding the identities of a film's actors and storylines before it can qualify for an Oscar. At the same time, Trader Joe's was in the news for defending itself against social media attacks charging the grocery chain with cultural appropriation because of the names of some of its products, like "Trader Jose" on some products inspired by Mexican cuisine, or "Trader Ming's" on its Chinese-inspired products. Red Bull was similarly criticized simply for not being more outspoken on social and political issues. Red Bull sells energy drinks.

Even the *New York Times*, once a trusted protector of journalistic freedoms, was in the news itself in 2020 after a social media eruption led to the resignation of its editor for giving space to a conservative politician. This was followed by the public resignation of columnist Bari Weiss, who claimed she was under constant ridicule and attack at the *Times* because of her moderately conservative views. "Showing up for work as a centrist at an American newspaper should not require bravery," Weiss wrote in her public letter of resignation.

As if on the precipice of Ray Bradbury's nightmare coming true, we routinely hear of book deals being canceled just before publication because of unfounded rumors and rage on social media. This is precisely what happened to the Young Adult science fiction writer Amélie Wen Zhao just before the debut of her book *Blood Heir* was canceled in response to preemptive claims of racism and cultural appropriation during a Twitter storm. Zhao's book is meant to be a metaphor highlighting the continued dangers of human slavery, trafficking, and exploitation around the world, written from her own perspectives as a Chinese immigrant to the U.S. As she said in a 2019 interview on NPR, "It snowballed into a lot of people who hadn't read the book, and there was just so much critique coming from people who hadn't read it. So that was really devastating to me because these are some real issues that draw from my background and from global issues that are ongoing and continue to affect so many people."[4]

As in the Medieval Dark Ages, a new social justice orthodoxy is increasingly forcing educators, artists, businesses, journalists, authors, politicians, and publishers to express everything through its narrowminded lens or else face the consequences of being blacklisted, banned, boycotted, cancelled, or otherwise punished. In contrast to this emerging period of Endarkenment, philosopher Bertrand Russell reminds us that the "Enlightenment was essentially a revaluation of independent intellectual activity aimed quite literally at spreading light where hitherto darkness had prevailed."[5] The good news about light is that it takes only the flicker of a small candle to overcome the night, only a spark of independent thought to shed light and illuminate minds.

If it is true, as Orwell imagined, that Endarkenment is accomplished "by cutting the language down to the bone," I will close by offering the following key for deciphering the true meaning behind much of the doublethink currently being expressed in Unitarian Universalism. I hope it sheds some light.

What they Say	*What they Mean*
ableist	freethinker
beloved community	obedient community
cooperation	compliance
covenant	dogma
doctrine of church	church doctrine
engage	obey
equality	sameness

equity	sameness
homophobic	freethinker
multiculturalism	segregation
mutual accountability	*we* will hold *you* accountable
racist	freethinker
refused to engage	refused to obey
reimagine	be ashamed
religious and spiritual	Christian, not humanistic
safe	close-minded
safe space	segregation
transphobic	freethinker
we	groupthink
anti-authoritarianism	disobedience
exceptionalism	outstanding
individualism	independence

"In the end the whole notion of goodness and badness will be covered by only six words—in reality, only one word." Obey.

---

[1] Herzog, William, R., *Jesus, Justice and the Reign of God*, Westminster John Knox Press, Louisville, KY, 2000, p. 173.
[2] Ibid., p. 153.
[3] Luke: 5:20
[4] "Amélie Wen Zhao On 'Blood Heir'", Lulu Garcia-Navarro, interviewer, *Weekend Edition Sunday,* November 17, 2019.
[5] Russell, Bertrand, *The Wisdom of the West*, ibid., p. 230.

APPENDIX A

Documents Pertaining to the Immediate Aftermath of the Publication of *The Gadfly Papers* & UUMA Censure

- March 21, 2018 – UUMA Censure of Rev. Richard Trudeau
- June 7, 2019 – Thank You Note from Meadville-Lombard Theological School
- June 22, 2019 – Public Statement from UUMA People of Color Indigenous Chapter
- June 22, 2019 – An Open Letter from White UU Ministers
- June 23, 2019 – Email to Eklof from UUA Co-Moderator During 2019 General Assembly
- July 10, 2019 – Meadville-Lombard Theological School Letter of Termination
- July 21, 2019 – Personal Email to Eklof Containing Explanation from Right Relations Team Member about Meeting with Eklof
- Aug. 16, 2019 – UUMA Letter of Censure
- Sept. 20, 2019 – Rev. Davis's Letter Seeking Clarification of UUMA's Censure Process
- Oct. 11, 2019 – UUMA Response to Rev. Davis's September Letter
- Oct. 30, 2019 – Social Media Post from UU Minister Reciting UUA & UUMA False Narrative about Eklof
- Nov. 12, 2019 – UU Ministers' Letter to UUMA Requesting a Conversation
- Nov. 22, 2019 – Email to Rev. Richard Davis from UUMA Board of Trustees in Response to UU Minsters' Request for a Meeting
- Dec. 10, 2019 – Attorney Letter to UUMA on Behalf of Eklof
- Jan. 10, 2020 – Rev. Davis's Official Response to UUMA Letter of Censure
- Jan. 29, 2020 – UUMA Letter of Reply to Attorney's Dec. 10 Letter
- Feb. 24, 2020 – Attorney Email Reply to UUMA
- March 6, 2020 – UU Church of Spokane Member Cover Letter & Resolution to UUA and UUMA

APPENDIX A

Reverend Richard Trudeau

Dear Richard,

At its meeting on March 21, 2018 the UUMA Board of Trustees voted to issue a letter of censure against you for conduct that violates our Covenant and Code of Conduct.

Specifically we found that you violated our Covenant in two areas:

- To support one another in collegial respect and care, understanding and honoring the diversity within our association;
- To use our power constructively and with intention, mindful of our potential unconsciously to perpetuate systems of oppression;

We further determined that you also violated our Ethical Standards within the Code of Conduct:

- I will demonstrate respect and compassion without regard to race, color, class, sex, sexual orientation, gender expression, age, physical or mental ability or ethnicity. Such equitable treatment shall be extended to all to whom I minister regardless of position in the organization, including to those who may disagree with me.
- I will work to confront attitudes and practices of unjust discrimination on the basis of race, color, class, sex, sexual orientation, gender expression, age, physical or mental ability, or ethnicity, and to challenge them within myself and in individuals, congregations, and groups I serve.

The Board took these actions as a result of complaints made against you on Facebook and in your chapter meetings. We hope that in receiving this admonishment from your fellow ministers you may take time to reflect upon how your words have been harmful to our colleagues, specifically women and colleagues of color.

This censure is a matter of counsel; it has no formal impact on your membership in the UUMA which you, of course, retain. However, please know that we will be in contact with your local chapter to ask how they will work to ensure that chapter meetings and retreats are truly open to, and minimally safe spaces for, UUMA members of all identities and backgrounds, and particularly for those with historically marginalized identities.

Signed,

The UUMA Board of Trustees

610 S. Michigan Avenue, Chicago, IL 60605 USA T: 1.773.256.3000 meadville.edu

APPENDIX A

Dear Todd —

Thank you for working with ▮ as his Teaching Pastor this year. Preparing seminarians for ministry is a huge task and it takes a team to give them the best chance for success. Meadville Lombard is grateful to have you as a teammate! Thank you for your support and your ministry.

In service, ▮

THE GADFLY AFFAIR

Public Statement: UUMA People of Color and Indigenous Chapter, Regarding *The Gadfly Papers*

June 22, 2019

Dear Unitarian Universalist Clergy:

We represent the chapter of the Unitarian Universalist Ministers' Association for ministers of color.

As we conclude a General Assembly reflecting on the Power of We, clergy of color are faced with the dissemination of racism, ableism, and the affirmation of other forms of oppression, including classism and homo- and transphobia, in a book called *The Gadfly Papers* by Todd Eklof.

We recognize that as Unitarian Universalist ministers, we choose, each and all, to commit to the UUMA Guidelines, which apply to this situation as follows:

- *I will demonstrate respect and compassion without regard to race, color, class, sex, sexual orientation, gender expression, age, physical or mental ability or ethnicity. Such equitable treatment shall be extended to all to whom I minister regardless of position in the organization, including to those who may disagree with me.*

- *I will work to confront attitudes and practices of unjust discrimination on the basis of race, color, class, sex, sexual orientation, gender expression, age, physical or mental ability, or ethnicity, and to challenge them within myself and in individuals, congregations, and groups I serve.*

The material in question lacks both respect and compassion, continually asserting that if people of color would only be logical, things would be different. Unfortunately, since racism is not logical, logic cannot be a primary tool in its resolution. The material goes on to single out a religious professional of color, ▇▇▇▇▇▇▇, as the cause of the problem of having to deal with racism, in a clear case of racialized bullying.

We, as ministers of color, reject the following:

1. The assertion that conflict concerning racism is a problem of faulty logic and can be addressed by logic.
2. The assertion that the faithful service of ▇▇▇▇▇▇▇ is the source of the problem. Her work has been the embodied practice of our liberation. We embrace the work of ▇▇▇▇▇▇ and other religious educators of color with a deep respect and gratitude.
3. The assertion that changes of heart and changes of practice will leave white Unitarian Universalists with less. All of us will benefit from the healing of our movement.

We call on our white colleagues to resist confusion and renew their dedication to the work of decentering white supremacy. We call on the UUMA to distinguish vitriol and destructive rhetoric from alternative constructive perspectives and, likewise, to enforce the UUMA guidelines. We are Unitarian Universalist ministers. We both belong with and co-create the Beloved Community.

In faith,

Your colleagues
UUMA People of Color and Indigenous UUMA Chapter

[39 signatories omitted]

APPENDIX A

June 22, 2019

With sadness and anger, we, the undersigned, join our voices with the chorus of Unitarian Universalists speaking up to name the harm caused by yesterday's release of *The Gadfly Papers: Three Inconvenient Essays by One Pesky Minister*, written and self-published by our colleague the Rev. Todd F. Eklof and distributed at the 2019 General Assembly in Spokane, Washington. As white ministers, we write today to make clear that this treatise does not represent us or our values, nor does it represent our vision for the ministry or for Unitarian Universalism. We deeply regret the harm this publication has already caused, and we know that this is another (intentionally provocative) incident that comes on the heels of months, years, generations of harm toward our colleagues of color. (We also acknowledge the harm in the treatise directed toward LGBTQ+ people, religious educators, people with disabilities, and others–many of whom are also people of color at the intersections of multiple identities.)

Rev. Eklof names the "sadness, fear, and anger I sometimes feel about what's going on in my religion" (p. 126) as one of his primary motivations for writing. We, too, have sadness, fear, and anger: sadness at the pervasiveness of harm being done to our members, religious professionals, and colleagues of color; our fear that the explosive resistance to facing white supremacy culture within our faith will cause even more harm; and our anger that the brilliance, compassion, power, and moral imagination of our people have yet again been channeled into responding to harm, rather than nurturing a truly liberatory Unitarian Universalism.

What, we wonder, would be possible if the creative energy of our leaders were freed up from reacting to instances of resistance and harm, and instead were channeled into imagining, building, and experimenting with practices that embodied the kind of liberation and wholeness that is the core yearning of our faith?

We recognize that a zealous commitment to "logic" and "reason" over all other forms of knowing is one of the foundational stones of White Supremacy Culture. Instead of accepting the frame of Rev. Eklof's arguments and debunking them, we instead affirm the following:

- **White Supremacy Culture (WSC) is alive and well within Unitarian Universalism.** The impacts of WSC are pervasive and harmful, and while all of us are spiritually harmed within such a dehumanizing system, the primary impacts fall upon people of color and Indigenous people (POCI). This treatise, itself, is a manifestation of WSC, and is causing harm to our siblings of color, as well as to the integrity of our ministry.
- **We believe our siblings of color as the experts in their own life experiences.** They have done the emotional labor of testifying, again and again, to the consistent marginalization, aggression, and traumatization that they experience in UUism, and are pleading with us to face and dismantle the systems and structures that enable such harm to continue. We are grateful for this painful truth-telling, which comes at great personal and professional risk, and affirm that we witness and believe their experiences, and commit to addressing harm. All politics are identity politics, and when the default is white supremacist patriarchy, we must trust the experience of those who are targeted.

- **When unjust power structures—and those who benefit from them—are exposed and critiqued, backlash is predictable.** We often conflate critiques of our behavior with condemnations of our personhood. Here, however, we affirm that Unitarian Universalist ministers must act in solidarity with those harmed by the power structures, while also unequivocally declaring that *although all people have inherent worth and dignity, all behaviors and ideas do not*. Ideas and language can indeed be forms of violence, and can cause real harm. It is disingenuous at best, and malicious at worst, to argue that those who have been targeted by systemic violence have an obligation to bear witness to "ideas and words" that demean and diminish their personhood and discount their lived experience. The predictable "freedom of speech" arguments are commonly weaponized to perpetuate oppression and inflict further harm.
- **Neither the perspectives espoused in this publication, nor the harmful process by which it was distributed, represent our understanding of competent, compassionate, courageous UU ministry.** As we continue the painful but necessary process of confronting WSC in Unitarian Universalism, white ministers are being asked to take a hard look at ourselves — individually, congregationally, denominationally — and to practice new and more liberatory ways of embodying our faith. A deep commitment to racial justice and dismantling white supremacy is a core competency of our calling as ministers, and those who cannot or will not commit to developing the musculature of resiliency, humility, and lifelong learning required may indeed find that UUism is no longer the appropriate home for their ministries. We plead with our white colleagues who are struggling to acknowledge the realities of WSC in our faith to remain at the table and lean into this work with us, with an open heart to transformation and repair.

We yearn for the day when Unitarian Universalism fully embodies the liberated and liberating promises of our theology, and we are committed to listening to the deep wisdom of those who have been pushed to the margins as they call us toward such a faithful future. And as we work toward that day, we, the undersigned white ministers, recognize that it is our responsibility to not only speak out against this particular harm and support processes of reparation and healing in its wake, but to actively recommit to the holy work of racial justice and dismantling all forms of oppression as a central spiritual discipline and praxis of our ministries.

In faith and solidarity,

[485 Signatures Omitted]

Names will continue to be added to the list of signers in the coming days. If you are a white Unitarian Universalist minister and would like to add your name to this list, please email rev.ashley.horan@gmail.com with your name, title, ministry setting, and location.

APPENDIX A

Todd Eklof

From:
Sent: Sunday, June 23, 2019 7:33 AM
To: minister@uuspokane.org
Subject: If you would like to return to GA spaces

Todd,

This email is to reiterate what I said to you via phone yesterday: you are welcome to participate in General Assembly events after you enter into an agreement with us about how you will uphold the covenantal commitments of our community at GA. This will require discussion and agreement with me as the Co-Moderator, and with representatives of the GA Planning Committee, about engaging at GA in keeping with the values and purposes of the GA gathering.

Please inform us in advance if you plan to return to the convention center or other GA spaces; respond to this email with the time and location that you will arrive, and we will meet you there so that we may seek to reach agreement.

In faith,

, MDiv, MCRE | Co-Moderator, Board of Trustees
Phone |
uua.org

July 10, 2019

Rev. Dr. Todd Eklof, minister
███████ Board President
Unitarian Universalist Church of Spokane
4340 West Fort Wright Drive
Spokane, WA 99224

Dear Rev. Dr. Eklof and ███████

Meadville Lombard Theological School regularly reviews its Teaching Pastor lists and the impact of our relationships with Teaching Congregations for the benefit of our students as they discern the journey towards fellowship. While we thank you for your willingness to be a Teaching Pastor and a Teaching Congregation we have decided not to continue this collaboration, effective immediately.

Sincerely,

Rev. ███████
Senior Director of Contextual Ministry

cc: Dr. ███████

APPENDIX A

Todd Eklof

From:	████████████████ >
Sent:	Sunday, July 21, 2019 12:26 AM
To:	Todd Eklof; ████████
Subject:	Whats this? Right on!

Todd,

This is ████. I am in the process of ████████████████ UUC. I boycott the GA each year because it is too damn expensive and everyone there seems to think ....(better not say). So I am sorry to make it to Spokane. I would've love to see you two again, and esp talk to you. Anyway ████████ Interim minister ████████ noted this in a recent newsletter:

One of the big surprises at GA was a three-essay text written and shared by the Rev. Todd Eckhoff, minister of the UU congregation in Spokane. This book slams the UUA, sides with a white, male mindset (those he feels are uncomfortable), and asks for a divorce from our association. ████ was aware of this text early, brought it to me, and offered me as a participant with the Right Relations team as they discussed this volume with the author. My role was, as it is, to be terribly hurt by Eckhoff's accusations, in part because they ignore the systemic oppression of people of color and the G, L, B, T, Q community in America and also due to the significant efforts at normalizing racial equity I witnessed in New Orleans prior to my arrival in Washington. Most grateful to ████ for being there, sizing up the situation, and knowing that I might be an appropriate older, white male who disagreed sharply with the views shared by Eckhoff. (I note that this minister has already withdrawn from the UU Minister's Association and was unwilling to enter into further discussions with representatives from the UUA.)

You see, I was a follower of a maverick minister, ████████ who was a pain in the neck for the UUA precisely because he criticized the UUA repeatedly. Also, as you may recall, I loved your book A Gospel for Liberals. So, despite what Rev ██ has to say agin your writings, and I am sure a lot of other UU Ministers agree, I stand with you. I applaud your courage, esp if you felt that you needed to withdraw from the The UUA's Minister Association, many of who seems to be stuck in Group Think....esp preceding the hosting of the GA. Must have been hard.

So, I am really sorry I haven't been by your way, as I would really love to talk some more about this. So I need to access your 3-essay text mentioned above. Where can I find it?

Hope all of you are doing well....esp healthwise. Again, would love to get together.
Thanks for all you do.

████

THE GADFLY AFFAIR

16 August, 2019

Rev. Dr. Todd Eklof
Minister, Unitarian Universalist Church of Spokane

Dear Todd,

As the leadership of the Unitarian Universalist Ministers Association, we are writing this letter of censure regarding the content and the manner of distribution (at the 2019 General Assembly) of your book, *The Gadfly Papers*. We hope this action will be received as an invitation into awareness, acknowledgment of the hurt that has been caused, and an opportunity for restoration, reconciliation, and engagement in the ongoing work of the UUMA, not as an attempted resolution of an "issue." The content of your book has caused great psychological, spiritual, and emotional damage for many individuals and communities within our faith. Because of the widespread impact, we are making this censure public and distributing it to all members of the UUMA.

As the continental leadership of the UUMA, our responsibility is to uphold our values and our covenant. We believe you have broken covenant. We write this letter to ask you to seek understanding of the harm that has been done and to work toward restoration. We would welcome the opportunity to help guide and support a public process of restoration, which we expect would foster widespread learning about what it means to be a covenantal faith.

We understand from your book that you want to encourage robust and reasoned debate about the direction of our faith. However, we cannot ignore the fact that logic has often been employed in white supremacy culture to stifle dissent, minimize expressions of harm, and to require those who suffer to prove the harm by that culture's standards. Further, we believe that dismissing testimonies of real people to the profound and pervasive pain of white supremacy culture and its many forms of oppression by simply categorizing them as *safetyism* or *political correctness* is both morally wrong and antithetical to our values as a faith tradition.

We believe that you have violated the spirit of the Ethical Standards in our Code of Conduct detailed in our Guidelines for the Conduct of Ministry, which call us to:
• Honesty and diligence in our work
• Respect and compassion for all people
• The work of confronting attitudes and practices of unjust discrimination on the basis of race, color, class, sex, sexual orientation, gender expression, age, physical or mental ability, or ethnicity in ourselves and our ministry settings.

As we call you to be accountable to your colleagues, we also call ourselves, as UUMA leadership, to be accountable to our members and to our covenant and values. We recognize that our current ethical standards leave room for ambiguity about what kinds of speech and behavior are racist and oppressive. Our commitment to the ongoing work to revise our Guidelines, clarifying expectations of anti-racist, anti-oppressive conduct in

Nurturing Excellence in Ministry
Unitarian Universalist Ministers Association
24 Farnsworth Street, Boston MA 02210 | P (617) 848-0416 | F (617) 848-0973

APPENDIX A

the practice of ministry, seems more crucial each day. We are also working to revise the accountability processes to ground them in values of justice, integrity, and healing rather than in their current legalistic frame.

It is our deepest desire, not to exclude people, but to welcome everyone into this work, recognizing that our members represent a wide spectrum of perspectives, experience, readiness, and willingness to engage. While we wish to be sensitive to that spectrum, we also must balance that against the stark and painful fact that people of color, indigenous, trans, disabled and other marginalized communities have testified over and over again to the spiritual, psychological, emotional, physical, and moral damage that racism and oppression have caused. Those impacts are not up for debate.

Grounded in our mission, with profound sadness for hurt that has been caused, and with deep longing for the promise of what can be, we close with this prayer of lament:

Spirit of Reason and Passion,
We hear again the cries of pain from those of marginalized identities
Pain inflicted all too often in the name of UU values and principles.
Their hope is dying, crushed once again by dismissal and devaluation
Is there room for all of us in this faith?
Yes, this is a faith for us all.
This is a faith where love is stronger than hate
Where justice is our mission and beloved community is our vision.
Where relationships are key to our individual growth and understanding.
We are a faith that balances mind and heart, and embraces both in spirit.
May we live into that balance.
Recognizing the power of our words to manipulate and harm,
May we remember the power of relationship,
And work toward restoration when covenant is broken.
Embraced by Love,
Striving towards Justice,
We pray.

Blessed Be

In faith,

The UUMA Board of Trustees and Executive Team

THE GADFLY AFFAIR

Dear UUMA Board Members,

As you may know, I'm currently serving as our colleague Todd Eklof's Good Officer. This is clearly the most challenging role I've taken on during my four terms as a Good Officer in the Pacific Northwest during the past 27 years of my ministry here.

There are many angles to this role, but for now I'd appreciate some clarification about your censure of him. I know you did not take this lightly, but I am quite confused about how this was done. If you could respond, as best you are able, to the questions below it would be very helpful.

Faithfully,

Rick Davis

=====================================

Questions for the UUMA Board of Trustees

1. What was the UUMA procedure under which this letter of censure was created? Or was it ad hoc?
2. Was the UUMA Board determination made on a purely subjective basis, or did it conform with published standards?
3. What is the intended (by the Board) effect of this letter of censure on Rev. Eklof? How is it intended/expected to affect his ministry in the future?
4. Has the UUMA issued other letters of censure (in recent years)? If so, were any of them based on ministerial beliefs?
5. The UUMA letter of censure states that Rev. Eklof has "broken covenant." Which specific elements of the covenant were the ones that were allegedly "broken?"
6. As UUMA ministerial members, are the individual members of the UUMA Board of Trustees also bound in covenant to the UUMA Guidelines?
7. Does there exist a process for revoking a letter of censure, if desired?
8. Who was the "concerned" (minister) party(s) who initiated this action (that resulted in this letter of censure)?
9. Were the minister(s)' concerns put in writing (thus converting it into a formal complaint)?
10. Did any such formal complaint describe the specific reasons for the concern and provide supporting evidence?
11. Does the "freedom of the pulpit" policy protect a minister from criticism of his/her views (from other UUMA ministers)?
12. Doesn't the freedom of the pulpit obligate UUMA ministers to speak truth as they see it? If so, was there a determination that Rev. Eklof's statements were not, in his view, truthful?

APPENDIX A

13. Did the minister(s) concerned about Rev. Eklof's views discuss their concern(s) with him (or with a Good Officer Person)?
14. Was the Continental Good Officer Person involved in this censure process? If so, how and when?
15. Was any such formal complaint provided to Rev. Eklof?
16. Was Rev. Eklof given the opportunity to examine any such complaint and respond to it?
17. Was UUMA's Committee on Ethics and Collegiality involved in evaluating any complaint against Rev. Eklof? If so, what actions did the Committee take?
18. Did the UUMA Board formally evaluate the complaint? If so, was this evaluation reflected in Board minutes?
19. Did the UUMA Board formally determine that the complaint was valid?
20. Is the UUMA board obligated to keep its evaluation of the complaint private (except to the involved parties)? And if so, why was the censure deliberately made public?
21. In making a determination to censure Todd, was the UUMA membership involved? If so, how and to what degree?
22. Do the UUMA Guidelines include provisions that protect a targeted minister from being falsely defamed (by other ministers)? If so, how is that protection provided?

[Emailed by Davis to UUMA September 20, 2019]

THE GADFLY AFFAIR

Todd Eklof

From: Richard Davis
Sent: Friday, October 11, 2019 4:03 PM
To: Todd Eklof; Terry Steichen
Subject: this just in from UUMA - response

Hi Todd and Terry,

This just came in - love to have you both parse this and help me discern next steps.

Thanks, rick

(PS - lots going on in my congregation this week, so I"m behind on looking at your emails Terry - try to catch up this weekend)

Dear Rick,

Thank you for your patience as I have been traveling and working with the Board to find the best way for us to respond to your questions. For a variety of reasons, answering your questions individually will be challenging, and we feel, not move the conversation forward. Rather, I will explain the context of the censure and the basis of it at large, in the hopes that might bring some clarity to the situation.

Some key points, as I see it, as the person who sits on the Board with the portfolio of policy.

1. The letter of censure was not a membership action. There seems to have been widespread confusion around this, and while I'm sure you understand this distinction, it still strikes me as a relevant point to make. This censure has no impact on Todd's membership in the UUMA; nor relevance to his Fellowship status with the UUA. It was and is a statement on the part of the Board that we as a body disapprove of an action that a member has taken. It is not a statement of censorship (another widespread confusion) or one that will prevent a member from speaking freely. It is a statement based on the reality that our actions have consequences. Since it was not a membership action, which is to say Todd's membership standing in the UUMA was not impacted by this action, the Board was neither required nor advised to follow the standards laid out in the Accountability Procedures in the Code of Conduct.
2. The authority for the Board to create such a letter of censure is laid out in the UUMA Guidelines for the Conduct of Ministry under the Section heading "A History of Guidelines and Its Revisions" which reads : "However, the UUMA takes these Guidelines seriously. Flagrant disregard of the Guidelines by ministers can be cause for censure or other disciplinary action by the Board of Trustees." The Board laid out in our letter of censure our views as to how Todd disregarded the Guidelines. There is no expectation nor requirement of confidentiality with a letter of censure within our documents, and others that have been made from various bodies of the UUMA have been both public and private.
3. We are a covenantal faith. As such, we, the Board of Trustees of the UUMA, are first and foremost responsible to the covenant of our organization. That covenant was voted on by the membership in 2009 and is available in the "Covenant" section of our UUMA Guidelines for the Conduct of Ministry. Each Board of Trustees carries the responsibility of interpreting the covenant to the best of their collective wisdom, and hopefully does so with integrity and faithfulness. We have done our best to do so in this case, and will continue to do so going forward.
4. We are intentionally working towards being an actively anti-oppressive, anti-racist faith as a whole, and as an association, this work is part of our mission. This is evidenced in the majority of our UUMA documents, has been voted on multiple times by the membership as a whole, and is part of our Policy statements as a Board. One of the truths of attempting to live as an anti-racist organization is that it is our job as leadership to center the voices of those who have, both in our association and in our country, sat too long on the margins. I

APPENDIX A

understand that it is different, it might not feel equitable, and that it seems as though the ground is shifting. It feels that way because the ground is shifting. And we are committed, as leadership, to doing our best to support that shift.

5. In reviewing your questions, it appears to me that several of them could be answered through a close reading of our governing documents, including the Bylaws and Constitution of the Unitarian Universalist Ministers Association and the UUMA Guidelines for the Conduct of Ministry. All of these are available on UUMA.org. The structure, bylaws and documents of the UUMA have shifted over the years, always with the vote of the membership (as is required by our Bylaws) and some of your questions indicated that reading the most recent copies would be helpful.

I hope these answers are useful to you, and if you would like to have further dialogue I would be happy to speak with you. My schedule has calmed down some so I hope it would be easier for us to find a time to connect. I would also invite you and Todd to engage with the Board as a whole through emailing us at ▉▉▉▉▉▉▉▉▉, or we can set up a Zoom call.

Thank you for your continued involvement as we wend through these difficult times. I appreciate your time, your commitment to our faith, and your kindness.

In Faith,
▉▉▉▉▉
- - -
Rev. ▉▉▉▉▉▉▉▉▉▉▉
Minister, ▉▉▉▉▉▉▉▉▉▉▉

Todd Eklof

From:	Pnwd-min ▇▇▇▇▇
Sent:	Wednesday, October 30, 2019 3:41 PM
To:	▇▇▇▇▇
Cc:	▇▇▇▇▇
Subject:	Re: [Pnwd-min] Gadfly papers, ▇▇▇▇▇

▇, Todd criticized specific religious professionals by name in his book. It's unfortunate that he didn't at any time seek their perspective on the situations he is so eager to weigh in on, before he dragged their names through the mud. Alas, in his echo chamber he only heard voices that agreed with him. Talk about not collegial…
My commitment to faith leadership means being accountable to my fellow religious professionals, ordained or not. ▇ is not in accountable relationships with colleagues. Despite numerous invitations from PNW ministers, UUA and UUMA staff, Todd refuses to meet with anyone who doesn't praise his text.
Who was it who said that if people took the God out of worship they would end up worshipping themselves?

▇▇

APPENDIX A

Request to the Board

Dear UUMA Board Colleagues,

This letter has been initiated by longtime UU ministers and joined by others of various tenures. While we ascribe to you no bad intentions, we believe your actions are an overreach of your authority and are in fact harmful to Unitarian Universalism and to the collegiality of the UU ministry.

We join the many voices, both clergy and laity that are expressing concern about your treatment of our colleague Todd Eklof, treatment that violates the collegial standards we have long agreed to live by. We are surprised and concerned that you unilaterally chose the confounding policy of censuring a colleague's writings, an action taken without due process: a formal complaint and an opportunity to answer it. Your reliance for authority to censure rests upon a single sentence in "A History of the Guidelines and Its Revisions," and is at best dubious.

We believe your actions violate our freedom of the pulpit, a freedom we believe extends to our writings. Those who initiated this letter find no violation of our covenant in Todd's book, only ideas which challenge particular approaches to anti-oppression currently in favor with many colleagues. All signatories believe that the changes you are making to our norms of ministerial collegiality and freedom of the pulpit are creating a deep divide amongst UU's and are resulting in an atmosphere of fear and distrust. Many good clergy are refraining from working together on common issues of importance, and long valued relationships are being damaged.

Our ethical standard is: *I will not speak scornfully or in derogation of any colleague in public. In any private conversation concerning a colleague, I will speak responsibly and temperately. I will not solicit or encourage negative comments about a colleague or their ministry.* This norm has been violated by the mass letters and your circulation of them. They were violated in subsequent online conversations in which, for example, Todd was compared to the Nazis at Charlottesville. UUMA moderators refused to intervene in these attacks on Todd and on anyone who defends his right to speak, as they normally would do in ad hominem attacks. Many signatures on the letters and on online attacks are coming from colleagues who have not even bothered to read Todd's essays.

To our knowledge, none of these colleagues have engaged Todd in conversation about their concerns. Thoughtful rebuttal is what we wish to see held up as the norm for discussions among colleagues and modeled to seminarians, not public slurs.

Some of us have served on the UUMA executive committee. We hope you would see as your fiduciary duty the calming of passions and the re-establishment of collegial norms. We hope you would remind colleagues that open conversations lead toward truth. Instead you chose one side of a debate among people of good will and used your position to censure a colleague you disagree with. You have increased anger and distrust and have even engendered despair among many of our colleagues. Your practice of bullying and silencing has severely damaged the collegial climate that once sustained us through difficult times. We trusted you to be our bulwark against the noxious national climate. This time of national turmoil is exactly the wrong time to back away from our collegial principles.

Ironically, your actions have discouraged dialogue on issues of race and other intersectional issues—issues we need to pursue in more depth by welcoming new approaches and new research. Fear and distrust make working together and working smarter far less likely.

Ibram X. Kendi in his book, How To Be an Anti-Racist, enjoins us who want to change racist policies not to blame those who do not accept our formulations, but rather to examine how well we are communicating. He says that blaming others for anti-racism failure, rather than being flexible and critiquing our own ideas, leads to further racism and further failure. He suggests that resistance from people with essentially divergent aims is an occasion for perseverance, whereas resistance from allies is an occasion for re-evaluation. The strong anti-racism record of many of us—and indeed of Todd himself—suggests that those who are critics of your actions are in the latter group. Rather than reviling colleagues who are not in agreement with

APPENDIX A

you, you would best follow Kendi's suggestion and use the pushback as a useful critique that gives information about how other progressives are viewing racial justice work.

Many ministers and other UU's of color feel that the mass letters and public condemnations are not only ineffective but even unethical. As these events become public, some laity are already responding extremely negatively to your actions, and we expect this response to only grow. We ask that you give up your ideological censure and categorical dismissal of colleagues who differ from you. We seek, rather, a return to tolerance for honest and openhearted sharing. We need leadership that will bring us together during this time of national threat, rather than dividing us and making us angry and fearful.

We ask you to engage with Rick Davis, Todd's good officer, along with a group of other experienced parish clergy of his choosing, with the goal of working in a climate of mutual respect towards a healthier stance, one that honors our collegiality and our traditions.

A commitment towards a just world does not require UU's to give up our core commitments to our liberal religious values and collegial practice—rather, this is the time for us to cling fast to our liberal religious values and refuse to support the current zeitgeist of blaming, fear, and division.

We write this letter in the collegial expectation of a quick response and the setting up of a meeting either on Zoom or face to face so that we might begin a process of reconciling our shared desire to move toward a more equitable world and at the same time maintaining our essential value of freedom of thought.

**[Sent to UUMA November 12, 2019
Signature of 63 ministers omitted]**

THE GADFLY AFFAIR

Todd Eklof

From:
Sent: Friday, November 22, 2019 8:07 PM
To: Richard Davis
Cc: Todd Eklof
Subject: checking in

Dear Rick,

I'm aware that since we last talked you had several questions for the UUMA's Board of Trustees. ▮▮▮▮ replied to your questions in mid October and my understanding is that she hasn't heard from you since.

In the recent "Request to the Board" letter that you and several other colleagues signed, Rick, one of your requests is for engagement with the Board. I'm writing tonight to underscore that the Board has desired and continues to desire the opportunity to engage.

Next week we expect to be able to share the Board's response to that "Request to the Board" letter. In that response, the Board plans to acknowledge that they are, in fact, eager to engage. The response will also state that they have authorized me to negotiate with you or with Todd to determine the parameters and participants of any meeting. As an act of good faith, I'm reaching out in advance of that response to let you know that meeting is a point of agreement and to see if we can begin to discuss the terms? If you and/or Todd would like to move forward in planning for a meeting, please let me know when and how you'd like to begin that work.

All my best,

Rev. ▮▮▮▮▮▮▮ | Director of Collegial Practices, member Executive Team, pro tem

Affiliated Minister, ▮▮▮▮▮▮▮, Unitarian

Unitarian Universalist Ministers Association

Nurturing Excellence in Ministry

Phone: ▮▮▮▮▮▮▮ | ▮▮▮▮▮▮▮

uuma.org | connect.uuma.org | facebook.com/uuministers | @UUMinAssoc

The UUMA is updating our email address system. Please note that as of Aug 22 my new email will be ▮▮▮▮▮▮▮. Thank you for updating your address book.

APPENDIX A

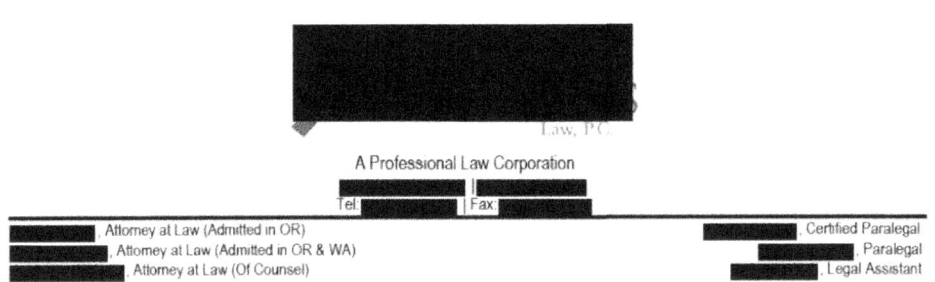

A Professional Law Corporation

_____, Attorney at Law (Admitted in OR)
_____, Attorney at Law (Admitted in OR & WA)
_____, Attorney at Law (Of Counsel)

_____, Certified Paralegal
_____, Paralegal
_____, Legal Assistant

December 10, 2019

_____
Unitarian Universalist Ministers Association
25 East Maple Street
East Hampton, MA 01027

Re: Procedural Due Process Regarding Censure Letter of the Rev. Dr. Todd Eklof

Dear Ms _____:

Please be advised that Rev Dr. Todd Eklof has asked me to review the strictly legal and contractual due process requirements the UUMA must follow prior to any formal member discipline such as a public letter of censure. This is without regard to the subject matter of the underlying issue.

Specifically, under the UUMA Code of Conduct the "Accountability Procedures" outlines a formal structural due process. After the initial informal steps of GOP involvement, the formal steps begin. To initiate my review, I hereby request copies of the following written documents as required under the UUMA "Accountability Procedures":

1) The written letter of complaint to the CEC,

   "...fully specifying the nature of concern making it a formal complaint."

2) If different, the written "formal grievance" the CEC forwarded to the UUMNA Board of Trustees pursuant to CEC Option 4.

3) Pursuant to UUMA Board Rule 3 a copy of the written "intent to act" that must be sent more than 30 days prior to the UUMA's meeting.

December 10, 2019

███████████

Re: Procedural Due Process Regarding Censure Letter of the Rev. Dr. Todd Eklof
Page 2

    4) If separate, the UUMA's Board letter informing Rev. Dr. Eklof of the meeting's time, date, location and expense reimbursement proposal also required more than 30 days prior to the meeting.

My request anticipates your full cooperation since UUMA Board Rule 4 states:

> "UUMA members shall have full access and full freedom and right to respond to all evidence against them."

Delivery may be by email attachments or US Mail to the following address:

███████████
Attorney at Law
███████████
███████████
███████████
███████████

Very Truly Yours,

███████████
███████████
Attorney at Law
███████

cc: 1) ███████████, President   2) Rev. ███████████,
    Unitarian Universalist Ministers Association
    ███████████

3) UUMA Board of Trustees   4) ███████████
   Unitarian Universalist Ministers Association   ███████eet
   24 Farnsworth St.
   Boston, MA 02210-1409

Email: ███████████ (+bcc)

APPENDIX A

To the UUMA Board of Trustee members (who signed the August 16, 2019 letter of censure of Rev. Dr. Todd Eklof)*:

Most regrettably, you have failed to adequately respond to our September 20th, 2019 written requests for clarity regarding your process and explicit reasons for your public censure of Rev. Dr. Todd F. Eklof. As I now have no expectation you will provide this, I am responding as his Good Officer based upon what we now know to be true.

1. **Harm to Rev. Eklof:** *You stated that your censure of Rev. Todd would not affect his UUMA membership nor his UUA fellowship, implying that it would not be harmful to him. That is obviously not true. The harm to him has been significant, is on-going and certainly was intentional on your part.*
2. **Breaking Covenants:** *The heart of your censure is an assertion, in the utter absence of evidence or specifics, that Rev. Eklof had "broken covenant." Based on covenants as they existed at the time (and as they still exist), that is simply not true. You even admit that in your letter of censure: "We recognize that our current ethical standards leave room for ambiguity about what kinds of speech and behavior are racist and oppressive." And this: "We are also working to revise the accountability processes.." And finally, you acknowledge that you consider Rev. Eklof's actions "..violated the spirit [rather than the letter] of the Ethical Standards in our Code of Conduct detailed in our Guidelines for the Conduct of Ministry.." In short, while you are seeking to revise existing Guidelines, you have no authority to preempt existing covenants in favor of those you seek to add.*
3. **Freedom of the Pulpit:** *Contrary to common sense, you state that your censure does not constitute any restriction on freedom of the pulpit or the freedom to of Rev. Eklof to "speak freely." That is obviously not true.*
4. **Violating Due Process:** *In a dismissive gesture, you assert authority to bypass ministers' long-standing rights of due process by inventively defining your "censure" process as something different from and not bound by, well-defined normal grievance procedures. That is false - you were given no such authority by the UUMA membership.*
5. **Unilateral Discretion:** *You also assert that you enjoy a fully discretionary (and apparently unreviewable) right to categorically approve or disapprove the actions of any minister. You have no such authority, unless it is self-endowed.*
6. **Covenantal Interpretation:** *You also assert the authority for unilaterally "interpreting the covenants," when the covenants are between ministers. That is false - you have no such authority.*
7. **Discrimination and Favoritism:** *While you assert authority to demand that Todd comport with some vague ministerial covenant, you are silent about the fact that these covenants equally apply to you, as UUMA minister members, and that your actions are in clear violation of them. And, you are also silent about applying them equally to the "white ministers" who wrote the June 22, 2019 "open letter" condemning Rev. Eklof.*
8. **Respect for Reason and Logic:** *You declare that, because arguments has been used by racists, that it is not a legitimate approach to expressing views. It's equivalent to saying that, because some crimes are committed with knives, knives are not legitimate instruments.*

For these reasons it is clear that you have failed in your duties as UUMA Board members, a failure which jeopardizes the integrity of the UUMA organization and its ability to carry out its important roles in supporting the UU ministry.

Your actions would be bad enough if your animosity only harmed Rev. Eklof. However, that's not the case. All UU ministers, whether or not they agree with the ideas Rev. Eklof expressed in his "Gadfly Papers" book, are now and in the future, at risk for similar unfair treatment if your false assertion of authority is permitted to go unchallenged.

We do agree with you that "We understand from your book that you want to encourage robust and reasoned debate about the direction of our faith." However, your actions demonstrate anything but a willingness for engaging in such a debate.

You say that you wish "..to welcome everyone into this work, recognizing that our members represent a wide spectrum of perspectives, experience, readiness, and willingness to engage.." Yet your actions completely and clearly bely those words.

We call upon you to honor the claim you made in your letter of censure that: ""We also call ourselves, as UUMA leadership, to be accountable to our members and to our covenant and values." To that end, because of the potentially broad implications of your actions regarding Rev. Eklof, we call upon you to distribute this letter to all of the UUMA member ministers (as you did in publishing your letter of censure, and your justification as laid out in your Censure Q&A). Our colleague ministers have a right to be aware of how your actions affect not just their colleague Todd Eklof, but potentially every one of them.

signed: Rev. Rick Davis, Good Officer

* These are: ███████, *President;* ███████, *Vice President;* ███████, *Treasurer;* ███████, *Member-at-Large;* ███████, *Member-at-Large;* ███████ *Member-at-Large;* ███████, *Director of Education;* ███████, *Director of Operations; and* ███████, *Director of Collegial Practice*

APPENDIX A

January 29, 2020

Mr. ███
Attorney at Law
███

Re: Rev. Dr. Todd Eklof

Dear Mr. ███,

This is in response to your December 10, 2019 request for certain UUMA documents regarding Rev. Dr. Eklof. As is apparent from the language of the letter we sent to Rev. Dr. Eklof dated August 16, 2019, that letter was not written in response to adjudication of a specific complaint. The UUMA Board was instead responding to the groundswell of concern that had been expressed by many UUMA members, as well as affiliated organizations.

The Board is not attempting to resolve a formal grievance, but rather inviting Rev. Dr. Eklof into a religious process of covenantal repair. We have extended repeated invitations to conversation to discern together a way forward that allows for us to come to a shared understanding and a pathway to restoration.

It is the Board's responsibility to uphold the Mission, Vision and the Code of the UUMA. After careful, prayerful discernment, we concluded a private formal reprimand was inadequate, both in response to the actions he took, and in the context of the public outcry from UUMA members.

As we are not following a formal structural grievance process, we are not including the documents you identified/requested. We remain open to entering into a process of reconciliation and restoration with Rev. Dr. Eklof.

Sincerely,
The UUMA Board of Trustees

Nurturing Excellence in Ministry
Unitarian Universalist Ministers Association
24 Farnsworth Street, Boston MA 02210 | P (617) 848-0498 | F (617) 848-0498

THE GADFLY AFFAIR

Todd Eklof

From:
Sent: Monday, February 24, 2020 10:28 AM
To:
Cc: UUMA Board
Subject: Re: UUMA Reply

Ms. ▮:

Thank you for your prompt response. I did not receive the formal UUMA Board response and must assume it was fully blocked by a spam filter. (Obviously not UUMA's fault)

It would appear that UUMA's formal position is that a nationally published formal "Public Letter of Censure" does not meet the threshold of a disciplinary proceeding.

In a nationally recognized case on the subject the Florida Supreme Court held that unlike social clubs:

"...a professional organization must observe due process and fairness required by Florida law in it's disciplinary proceedings, and that the Ethics Committee failed to adhere to fair standards set out in it's own procedural regulations in acting against petitioner in that the Committee failed to give fair and adequate notice, failed to give notice of charges with adequate particularity, and otherwise failed to provide a fair and impartial hearing."

See McCUNE v. WILSON, et. al., 237 So. 169, (1970), page 170.

I assume you were advised by legal counsel whether a nationally published letter of censure met this threshold.

I therefore urge you to have your legal counsel contact me directly to discuss this legal "red line". In the meantime I will advise Rev. Dr. Eklof to collect all evidence of the impact on his life this letter produced.

Of course, since the UUMA's position is that nothing formal happened this opens the door for libel. (That Rev. Dr. Eklof is Guilty of "broken covenant", employed white supremacy logic, violated the spirit of the "Ethical Standards of our Code of Conduct", including that of dishonesty, and so on)

APPENDIX A

The UUMA cannot simply avoid due process by recategorizing outside it's own due process rules without entering the libel arena.

But this is why I want to discuss all this with your legal counsel. Have them email me, we can set a phone appt. and then go from there.

THE GADFLY AFFAIR

March 6, 2020

Spokane WA. Unitarian Universalist Members
4340 W. Ft. G Wright Drive
Spokane, WA 99224

UUMA Board of Directors
UUA Board of directors
24 Farnsworth St.
Boston, MA 02210

We the members of the Unitarian Church of Spokane respectfully submit the enclosed resolution for your consideration. We are gravely concerned about the direction our association is heading, particularly by stifling descent. Please receive this resolution as our call for a return to civility and our traditional liberal religious values.

203 UUCS Members and Friends

[Signatures Omitted]

APPENDIX A

We, the undersigned members and friends of the Unitarian Universalist Church of Spokane, put forth this resolution to the UUA and the UUMA in response to their reaction and its subsequent impact on our congregation following the writing and release of our minister's most recent written work, "The Gadfly Papers":

- We believe UUCS is a welcoming community, where diversity of thought, ideas, ways of being and knowing are our strengths—not a source of division.

- We view our congregation as healthy and vibrant as evidenced by active and engaged members and friends doing meaningful work, both within our cherished walls and outside in the wider community.

- We believe that the censure of ideas is antithetical to who we claim to be. We not only support our minister's right to freedom of conscience and freedom of the pulpit, on both the local and national level, we *expect* him or her to uphold our bylaws and principles using evidence and reason, as we each are challenged daily with our own *free and responsible* search for truth and meaning.

    - We believe Rev. Todd Eklof acted with great courage. Whether we agree with his ideas in "The Gadfly Papers "or not, we respect his right to raise concerns and to be heard. We stand resolutely with him as he continues to suffer the consequences for taking personal and professional risks in upholding core principles of Unitarian Universalism.

- In challenging times, we will interact with each other openly and respectfully, keeping in mind our shared goals and historical values that have guided UUCS forward for more than a century.

- Lastly, and perhaps most importantly, we will continue to honor our individual freedoms even as we deeply understand that it is our common humanity, paired with rationality, that are essential to living in a sane and just world.

203 UUCS Resolution Signatures
(f) indicates friend

APPENDIX B

Documents Pertaining to UUMA Concerns Regarding the Role of Rev. Rick Davis as Good Officer and the Eventual Removal from the Post

- Aug. 27, 2019 – Personal Email from Rev. Richard Davis Regarding Continuing UUMA Communications about His Role as Good Officer
- Sept. 11, 2019 – UUMA Concern Over Rev. Davis's Intention to Preach Sermon about His Role as Good Officer
- Sept. 25, 2019 – Personal Email from Rev. Davis Regarding Continuing Good Officer Concerns Being Expressed by UUMA
- Sept. 30, 2019 – Rev. Davis's Response to UUMA Criticism of his Role as Good Officer
- April 2, 2020 – UUMA Letter Notifying Rev. Davis of His Termination from Good Officer Program
- April 13, 2020 – Rev. Davis's Letter of Response to UUMA Regarding His Termination from Good Officer Program

APPENDIX B

Todd Eklof

From:	Richard Davis
Sent:	Tuesday, August 27, 2019 7:13 PM
To:	Todd Eklof
Subject:	update from rick d

Brother Todd - here's what I got from ▮ today - I'm open to chatting with her, but want to hear your thoughts before I do. (see below in blue)

FYI: My posts on the Gadfly Paper FB page to which she refers were simply to affirm that I support you right of conscience and free expression, that I am dismayed by the letter and the censure and exploring how to respond, and I've weighed in a couple of times when I felt it was helpful. I have also encouraged the UU lay folks to let the UUA and UUMA know of their displeasure (most folks on this page are in fundamental agreement that this whole fiasco impinges upon fundamental freedoms enshrined in our tradition. There are some very open and interesting discussions there).

Folks are also wondering what I'm up to and I have said that I am moving slowly and discerning my next step, which you and I are. That may be why ▮ and another anonymous Good Officer say I seem to be "struggling." I call it discerning. My latest effort is to explore the process for having the entire UUMA membership weigh in on the censure as we talked about on the phone.

I do appreciate that ▮ affirms my right to act as my conscience dictates, and I hope she can shed some light on good ways to proceed, but we can't forget that her name is on the letter of censure.

Your thoughts? (As always, if you don't have time to respond quickly, it's OK.

Take care!
rick

Hi, Rick,

A fellow good officer noticed your posts on the Gadfly Facebook page and emailed me concerned that you seemed to be struggling to clarify your role. I joined the group and am currently wading through. I've come across a couple of your comments so far, and I, too, think I hear some struggle??

Anyway, I figured I would reach out, this time with my official formerly-known-as-continental-good-officer hat on, to request a conversation. All Good Officers wear different hats in different situations, and it is tricky to discern the role we are meant to play when we are accompanying a colleague through the accountability process. You will, of course, have to act as your conscience dictates, but perhaps it would be helpful to you to hear what I understand about the process and the most productive way for GO's to participate in it. Having counseled and debriefed many of our GO colleagues who have done this work, as well as having been in the role myself, I may be a good sounding board.

This is challenging work, and these are complicated times.

Yours in faith and friendship,

▮

THE GADFLY AFFAIR

Todd Eklof

From: Richard Davis
Sent: Wednesday, September 11, 2019 7:22 PM
To: minister@uuspokane.org

Brother! Look what just arrived in my inbox (see below). Like to chat with you before I have this conversation with ▇▇▇▇ I can chat tonight, tomorrow at 9 to 9:30 or around noon or evening. Not sure about the lay of the land here and if they can remove me from Good Offices or not. So, let's chat. See ya, rick

Dear Rick,

I am writing today as it has come to my attention that you are planning to preach a sermon later this month regarding the controversy surrounding the Gadfly Papers. My understanding is that you are serving as Todd Eckloff's Good Officer. If that is correct, I'm concerned that preaching on the Gadfly conflict may compromise your ability to serve in the Good Offices role for Todd. I'd like to speak with you about this and make sure you understand current expectations of Good Officers. When might you have some time?

I'm copying ▇▇▇▇▇▇▇▇ as she is the UUMA Board of Trustees member who holds the portfolio for Counsel and Advocacy and, in that role, works with me to oversee the ministry of Good Offices. If you like, ▇▇▇▇ can join us for our conversation.

All my best,
▇▇▇▇

APPENDIX B

Todd Eklof

From:	Richard Davis
Sent:	Wednesday, September 25, 2019 10:37 PM
To:	Todd Eklof
Subject:	from rick d - two latest emails from UUMA board members

Brother - My two latest emails from UUMA board members - cut and pasted below. We can chat about this. Always like to get your perspective before I engage. Hope you are well!
rick

Dear Rick,

I read your sermon on Gadfly, and I'm writing again to request a conversation. I know you have consulted widely and discerned carefully, but I wonder if you have spoken with someone who's been a part of the accountability process in the last five years?

The way formal grievances are handled has really shifted, and the good officer has a particular role to play in the process. I am very concerned that your public statements seriously compromise your ability to fulfill that role, which would require you to recuse yourself should someone initiate the accountability process. While the letter of censure isn't the same as the filing of a formal grievance, there are bound to be some parallels. This could wind up doing Todd a major disservice.

If you're not comfortable talking with me (which breaks my heart, as we've known each other for more than 15 years) I can give you a list of a few other possible contacts. I know this must be incredibly hard for you. It is no walk in the park for me, either.

I believe we share the same goal, though- learning, discernment, and a repair of relationship and restoration of covenant. We can differ as to the 'how', but please keep the goal in mind. The best path is almost always found somewhere between the two extremes.

With love, in faith and friendship,

Hi Rick,
I would be happy to schedule time for us to connect and talk through your questions about the guidelines, censure and policies. I hope I can be helpful. Tomorrow is pretty full, but Friday is my writing day and I could take out some time to visit with you if that might work? I also have time on Monday morning while I'm driving, but will not have access to our documents at that time, so won't be able to give you as clear citations if that's important for you. I'm out of town at a meeting from Monday to Wednesday, but then have some availability the following Friday if that might work as well? If none of these times are convenient for you, please let me know what might be good and I'll do my best to adjust accordingly.

Looking forward to speaking with you.

Warmly,

THE GADFLY AFFAIR

Todd Eklof

From:	Richard Davis █████████
Sent:	Monday, September 30, 2019 4:38 PM
To:	Todd Eklof
Subject:	from rick d - note to ██████ - you OK with this?

Brother - about to send this to █ per her request for a conversation. You OK with this? Would like to send it soon. Hope all is well! rick

Note to ████████

Hi █,

I know you'll be disappointed to read this, but I have decided that having a conversation with you will have to be put on hold. Right now I am in communication with another member of the UUMA board in regards to the censure and that requires my full attention. I need more clarity on the process by which that was done.

I can tell from our communication that we have some fundamental disagreements, also I also sense that the time is not ripe for true dialogue. To have dialogue, there needs to be a humble willingness for all parties to listen and grow through the experience. So far, all I have seen from the UUMA is the desire for a monologue in which the UUMA does all the talking and Todd does all the listening. That won't work. In fundamentalist religions they contend that there is only one true religion – the fundamentalist's religion. Here it seems that there is only one true opinion – the UUMA's opinion. That's very disturbing to me.

You have expressed concern that my public advocacy is doing Todd a disservice which you fear could lead to a grievance being filed against him and that this would be more consequential than the censure (which you signed). I can't imagine what kind of grievance could be filed against him for honestly sharing his views, but if one comes, we will have to face that. I have consulted with Todd about this and he agrees with me.

My honest view is that what Todd needs and deserves is support for exercising his freedom of conscience and expression in his ministerial role – that is a hallmark of our liberal religion and is affirmed in our UUMA guidelines. I support this right for everyone, whether they agree or disagree with me. I realize there is more nuance to this argument where historically marginalized people are concerned, and I am open to listening and learning more in the future, as is Todd.

█, this matter is larger than our personal relationship which I fear is being damaged. I never wanted us to come to this impasse, yet I have seen this coming ever since I negotiated the resignation of ████████ in my role as Good Officer. It struck me then that shortcuts were taken that subverted due process. The final communication from the UUMA to █ was shocking to me in its severity. I was afraid to speak out then because I was afraid of the response – indeed, I think that such is the climate of fear and intimidation that many colleagues are now afraid to share their honest views. That's not a good thing.

My hope and prayer is that the day will come when we be able to resolve all of this and reflect on what we have both learned. I know you think I'm making a terrible mistake here, but I do not. If I am wrong, I will be honestly wrong and will be open to new learning. Todd feels the same way.

APPENDIX B

May the light, love and truth of the sacred mystery guide us both as we make our way through this difficult passage in our journey.
rick

2 April 2020

Dear Reverend Richard R. Davis,

I am writing today to inform you that we are removing you from the UUMA's list of Ratified Chapter Good Officers effectively immediately. I'm copying the President, Treasurer, Secretary and Collegiality and Ethics Portfolio holder from your chapter leadership on this communication that they might reconsider your suitability to serve as an elected Good Officer for your chapter.

Over the last several months, you have repeatedly violated the boundaries of the Good Offices role. The role of the Good Officer, as described in the Good Offices Handbook, includes providing counsel and support. In the case of conflicts that require written negotiation of terms, agreements or covenants or the termination of a relationship, the role may include representation.[1] The Handbook also references the UUMA Code of Conduct, which defines the role of the Good Offices person as "initially neutral, advising the member, and exploring the possibility of an informal resolution of the concern."[2] Further, the Handbook specifically states that "the role does not include being either judge or advocate."[3] These expectations were reinforced in the 2018 Good Offices Training session.

You have consistently and publicly advocated in support of the minister in your care, Rev. Dr. Todd Eklof, despite my counsel in November 2019 against publicly taking a position. I expressed to you in our conversation that public advocacy is inappropriate for a Good Officer and that you ran the risk, if you continued in that vein, of undermining your capacity to serve in the prescribed manner. To be specific, I am aware that you have advocated in support of Rev. Dr. Eklof through your communications with and preaching within at least two congregations: the Unitarian Universalist Church of Spokane, WA and the Unitarian Universalist Church of Salem, OR. The recent public statement to the UUA and the UUMA on the matter, from the President of the Board of Trustees of the

---

[1] Good Offices Handbook, pages 5 and 6.
https://www.uuma.org/global_engine/download.aspx?fileid=F360ABAB-3D89-4457-A411-FE6D43463CE2&ext=pdf
[2] Ibid, page 29.
[3] Ibid, page 34.

Nurturing Excellence in Ministry

Unitarian Universalist Ministers Association
24 Farnsworth Street, Boston MA 02210 | P (617) 848-0498 | F (617) 848-0498

congregation you serve, demonstrates that you have led the congregation to study and take a position on the conflicts you are charged to help Rev. Dr. Eklof address.

Of course, we cannot prevent Rev. Dr. Eklof from continuing to rely upon your support and counsel and we cannot prevent you from acting as his advocate. He is free to consider you his Good Officer. The UUMA, however, no longer recognizes you as authorized to fulfill that role.

Sincerely,

Rev. ███████████
Director of Ministries for Collegial Care

THE GADFLY AFFAIR

April 13, 2020

▉▉▉▉▉▉▉▉▉ Director of Collegial Relations
UUMA Board of Trustees

I have received your letter in the midst of a historic pandemic which has compelled me to focus all my energies on meeting the many challenges this poses for the congregation I serve and all our congregations. During this time of a global health care crisis your letter seems especially ill timed. Nevertheless, I must respond.

It has been my privilege and honor to have been elected by my colleagues to serve four terms (two 4 year terms and two 3 year terms) as a Good Officer in the PNW Chapter of the UUMA over the past quarter century. I will continue to offer support and counsel to those colleagues who seek it from me.

Most importantly, I must respond to the dubious assertions in your letter.

During the UUA General Assembly of 2019 I became aware that a colleague, Rev. Todd Eklof, was being publicly condemned in a harsh letter signed by 300 *(soon to be 500)* colleagues as a consequence of sharing his honest, heartfelt views in his book "The Gadfly Papers…" *(which gives voice to views shared by many Unitarian Universalists)*. I was dismayed when you, the Director of Ministries for Collegial Care and the rest of the UUMA Board, did you not step in and remind them of our UUMA Code of Ethics which clearly states *"I will not speak scornfully or in derogation of any colleague in public. In any private conversation concerning a colleague, I will speak responsibly and temperately. I will not solicit or encourage negative comments about a colleague or their ministry."* Nor did you guide these many colleagues to observe the processes outlined in our UUMA Guidelines for registering their concerns.

Instead of guiding these colleagues toward spiritually grounded, covenantal ways for communicating their concerns—ways that could have created the opportunity for dialogue and mutual learning—you stepped aside while many attacked Rev. Eklof in person, print and from the pulpit. Then, you soon joined in, publicly censuring his book without the due processes outlined in our UUMA Guidelines. You have misused and abused the power entrusted to you to ensure fair treatment of Rev. Eklof.

In the midst of this harsh and damaging public condemnation of Rev. Eklof, which you enabled and amplified by your public censure, you warned me that I must remain publicly silent while Rev. Eklof continued to be publicly judged, tried and sentenced by those who categorically condemned his book without attempting to engage him in honest dialogue.* Had our UUMA safeguards been in place to protect Rev. Eklof from this humiliating spectacle I would not have been compelled to speak out.

You claim I transgressed boundaries when I "advocated for Todd." In fact, I have not "advocated for Todd," rather I have advocated for the principle he was practicing, one that lies at the core of our free faith tradition, freedom of conscience and expression. The fact that my speaking in favor of these principles from the pulpit has proven to be at all controversial

APPENDIX B

indicates that we are experiencing a very serious threat to democratic principles that lie at the very foundation our movement. Such a threat calls for the attention of all Unitarian Universalists.

You further state, without any first hand knowledge, that I led my congregation to study and take a position on this conflict. This is both condescending toward the members of the congregation, who are quite capable of thinking for themselves, and false. It was their own process of dialogue and collective discernment, which I neither initiated or participated in, that led them to to send letters to the UUMA and the UUA. *(I daresay that many Unitarian Universalists would register similar concern were they but aware of what is transpiring within our movement or were they not intimidated by the climate of fear and intolerance you have helped create.)*

Indeed, had I not spoken out as I have during this past year I would inwardly know myself to be the rankest of hypocrites. Why? Because I have spent my entire ministerial career—34 years serving two wonderful congregations—preaching, teaching, being present with them in the spirit of love all while nurturing the understanding that we honor one another's freedom of conscience and expression. It's a matter of mutual spiritual respect. This principle lies at the heart of our free faith tradition, and I would be unfaithful to my calling were I not to defend it. So often over the years of my ministry I have reminded myself and others that we are called to be true to ourselves and others, and that when we disagree we enter into mutually respectful dialogue. The freedom to do this is sacred. To deny this freedom to an individual is to nullify their being. To deny this freedom within our movement is to extinguish the flame of our free faith.

Most Sincerely,

Rev. Rick Davis

Rev. Rick Davis

*re: "honest dialogue": After the censure, not before, Rev. Eklof and I were invited to encounters that were characterized as opportunities for dialogue. This is disingenuous. Dialogue is grounded in mutual respect and holds out the promise of mutual transformation and growth. Instead, you refused to honestly engage with us and respond to our questions about your censure.

APPENDIX C

Documents Pertaining to LREDA Complaint Against Eklof & His Excommunication by the MFC

- Jan. 8, 2020 – MFC Letter Announcing LREDA Complaint & Investigation
- Jan. 8, 2020 – LREDA Complaint
- Feb. 4, 2020 – Initial Communication from MFC Investigator
- Mar. 3, 2020 – MFC Request for Eklof Interview
- Mar. 5, 2020 – Davis/Eklof Initial Response to MFC Indicating Unwillingness to Participate
- Mar. 6, 2020 – MFC Reply and Reminder of Rule 28
- Mar. 11, 2020 – Eklof Reply to MFC Reiterating Unwillingness to Participate
- Mar. 11, 2020 – MFC Reply Stating, "Well received."
- Mar. 30, 2020 – MFC Letter Stating It Is Moving Forward Based on Violation of Rule 28 and Inviting Questions
- Apr. 23, 2020 – Rev. Davis Email to MFC Containing Davis/Eklof Response to March 30 Communication
- Apr. 23, 2020 – Letter to MFC Containing Davis/Eklof Statements Regarding its Continuing Investigation, Including Several Questions
- Apr. 24, 2020 – Reply from MFC Stating, "Well received" and Further Promising to Review "your questions, confer with MFC, and get back with you."
- May 21, 2020 – MFC Letter Stating it Will Convene on June 5th to Consider Eklof's Removal from Fellowship
- May 26, 2020 – Reply from Davis/Eklof Regarding MFC's Intention to Move Forward without Having Responded to Questions and Concerns
- June 7, 2020 – Letter from MFC Announcing Eklof's Disfellowship (Excommunication)
- June 9, 2020 – Email from UUMA Notifying Eklof his UUMA Membership has been Revoked
- Sept. 15, 2020 – "We Quit" Letter from 13 UU Ministers Withdrawing Their Membership from the UUMA

APPENDIX C

January 8, 2020

The Rev. Dr. Todd Eklof
Unitarian Universalist Church of Spokane
4340 W Ft G Wright Dr.
Spokane, WA 99224-5275
minister@uuspokane.org

Dear Todd –

I'm writing to you in my role as the Executive Secretary of the Ministerial Fellowship Committee to let you know that the UUA has received a complaint of ministerial misconduct against you from the board of the Liberal Religious Educators Association. The complaint is attached. You will see that it addresses four areas of the UUMA Code of Conduct:

1. *I will be honest and diligent in my work to fulfill the offices of ministry according to the stipulations of my call or employment and my best professional judgment.*
2. *I will demonstrate respect and compassion without regard to race, color, class, sex, sexual orientation, gender expression, age, physical or mental ability or ethnicity. Such equitable treatment shall be extended to all to whom I minister regardless of position in the organization, including to those who may disagree with me.*
3. *I will work to confront attitudes and practices of unjust discrimination on the basis of race, color, class, sex, sexual orientation, gender expression, age, physical or mental ability, or ethnicity, and to challenge them within myself and in individuals, congregations, and groups I serve.*
4. *I will not engage in public words or actions that degrade the vocation of ministry or diminish among us the esteem of our calling.*

Per MFC procedure the matter has been assigned for an initial investigation to one of our Consultants for Ethics and Safety, the ▓▓▓▓▓. The ▓▓▓▓▓ will be in touch with you to discuss next steps.

In the meantime, I would suggest that you share this complaint with a Good Officer for collegial support and counsel. It may be helpful to review the MFC Rules 20-28, and Policy 17 which govern complaint cases for ministers in final fellowship. Please note especially Policy 17 c. which states in part: *Confidentiality is key to the complaint process, and all parties are asked to respect the sensitivity of the information generated.* Therefore, do not share this complaint with anyone beyond your immediate family and closest trusted friends/advisors. Please do not publicly post about this complaint on social media.

If you have any questions about the process, The Rev. ▓▓▓ can answer those for you at this point. Once she has completed her interviews and review of the matter, she will make a recommendation about whether this matter is appropriate for a fellowship review with the Ministerial Fellowship Committee. If the case does get forwarded to the MFC, I will be your point of contact for that process.

MFC policies require that I inform the board president of your congregation that an investigation has been initiated regarding a misconduct complaint. I will cc the Rev. ███████ as the primary contact for your congregation, so that she can provide guidance and support for the congregation during this challenging time.

In peace,

The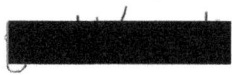
Executive Secretary, Ministerial Fellowship Committee
Co-Director of Ministries and Faith Development

Cc: The Rev. ███████ ; The Rev. ███████ ; the Rev. ███████ , Chair MFC.

APPENDIX C

Liberal Religious Educators Association
13036 SE Kent-Kangley Road Ste. 365
Kent, WA 98030

UUA Office of Ethics and Safety
24 Farnsworth Ave
Boston, MA 02210

Dear UUA Office of Ethics and Safety

This complaint is filed on behalf of members of the 2017-18 LREDA Board and the current (2019-20) LREDA Board against Rev. Todd Eklof, Minister, Unitarian Universalist Church of Spokane. This complaint concerns Rev. Eklof's self-published book, "The Gadfly Papers", released in the spring of 2019. In the book, his description of the events of the 2017 LREDA Fall Conference is filled with factual errors, misleading statements, and innuendos. He establishes a pattern of offering "evidence" to solely support his views by cherry picking events and quotes, and misrepresenting what people said and did. Eklof failed to demonstrate any diligence in pursuit of the truth of what happened at the conference. His conduct failed to demonstrate respect and compassion to all people, or investigate and confront attitudes and practices of unjust discrimination.

Background

In 2017, the LREDA Board and Fall Conference Planning Team brought ▇▇▇▇▇▇ and ▇▇▇▇▇▇ to be the featured speakers at the 2017 LREDA Fall Conference. Their presentation was found by the LREDA leadership to embody white supremacy and patriarchy, and the impact of their actions brought pain for conference participants of color, transgender people, survivors of abuse and others. As a result, the speakers' presentation was suspended early on the second day of the conference and ▇▇▇▇▇ and ▇▇▇▇▇ were paid in full and asked to leave.

Complaint

As author of 'The Gadfly Papers', we believe Rev. Eklof's conduct violates the Ethical Standards in the UUMA's Code of Conduct detailed in the Guidelines for the Conduct of Ministry as follows:

Specific areas of concern under the UUMA Code of Conduct:
Ethical Standards
1. "I will be honest and diligent in my work to fulfill the offices of ministry according to the stipulations of my call or employment and my best professional judgment."

2. I will demonstrate respect and compassion (to all people) without regard to race, color, class, sex, sexual orientation, gender expression, age, physical or mental ability or ethnicity. Such equitable treatment shall be extended to all to whom I minister regardless of position in the organization, including to those who may disagree with me.
3. I will work to confront attitudes and practices of unjust discrimination on the basis of race, color, class, sex, sexual orientation, gender expression, age, physical or mental ability, or ethnicity, and to challenge them within myself and in individuals, congregations, and groups I serve.
4. I will not engage in public words or actions that degrade the vocation of ministry, or diminish among us the esteem of our calling.

Evidence of Violations

(All citations are from: *The Gadfly Papers, Three Inconvenient Essays by One Pesky Minister* by Todd F. Eklof, independently published, Spokane, WA 2019 by Todd F. Eklof. We have 2 different hard copies of the book. Occasionally a paragraph of the book that we cite below, appears on different pages in the two different books. When that is the case, both pages are noted.)

1.

As demonstrated below, Rev. Eklof assumes that the reason the two presenters at the 2017 LREDA Fall conference were called out as embodying white supremacy was because they were white men, not for their actions. But Rev. Eklof elected to interview only the two offending speakers from the LREDA 2017 Fall Conference and one unidentified LREDA conferee who "found it hard to understand" what the speakers had done wrong. Apparently, Eklof made no attempt to investigate why the actions of the presenters had negatively impacted people of color and others. Instead he took the word of the presenters that they had done nothing.

- P. 40 "More troubling, however, is that ▇ letter of explanation (November 8th, 2017) defamatorily referred to the two men as speakers that embodied white supremacy and patriarchy."
- p.42 "These preconference communications prove beyond doubt that some were upset before ▇ and ▇ ever spoke a word, not because of anything they could have said, since they hadn't yet said anything, but simply because they are "white and male," and, for this reason alone, [all underlining of cited quotes from "The Gadfly Papers" in this complaint is LREDA's emphasis added] as ▇ letter of explanation explicitly concludes. they "embodied white supremacy and patriarchy."
- p.42 "My intention here is only to point out ▇ and ▇ likely did nothing worthy of such disrespect and indignity, and, likewise, could have done nothing to prevent it. Theirs was an original sin, the congenital condition of having been born both "white and male."
- p.44 "Their supposed offence, rather, as has been firmly established, was being "white and male," the "embodiment of white supremacy and patriarchy," and for this reason alone, some believe, should not have been allowed to have a presence at the event, nor even have their offensive images presented in its promotional materials."

At no time did Rev. Eklof interview or reach out to President ▇ or any other LREDA Board member, staff, or Fall Conference planning team member. By not interviewing these people, any persons of color, or others who were impacted, Rev. Eklof violated the UUMA's

APPENDIX C

Ethical Standards on demonstrating respect and compassion for all people regardless of position in the organization, and on being honest and diligent in his work.

Additionally, by not interviewing anyone except the two white males who are accused of white supremacy and one unidentified conferee who was unfamiliar with how white supremacy presents itself, his actions not only failed to confront attitudes and practices of unjust discrimination but were also in fact racist.

Not fully investigating or even conducting minimal research on the opposing view fails to meet minimal standards of diligent work.

We note that Rev. Eklof uses the term "Witch Hunt" as the heading of this section (P. 37). A witch hunt is known to be an unfounded targeting of individuals based not on fact but on assumption. Instead of confronting attitudes of unjust discrimination, as the UUMA Code of Conduct requires, he is promoting unjust discrimination. He has written opinions based on his own assumptions, rather than well-researched facts, misrepresenting what happened at the conference.

2.
Rev. Eklof claims the disruption of the presenters' program was pre-planned. Again, his allegation is based on assumption not fact. Nothing about the early dismissal of the two conference speakers was pre-planned. There was nothing on the LREDA website, or within the LREDA or UU Religious Educators Facebook groups calling for disruptive action at the conference.

- P. 39, "what seems fated to have occurred at the LREDA Conference" [implying that the presenters' dismissal was "pre-planned"]
- P. 41, " says he was also informed the entire ruckus had been part of a setup, 'This is not an accident. This was preplanned,' he was told: 'There was a lot of stuff on social media organizing this disruptive action, and that it was organized and planned.' So there really was nothing we could do." Such proof, it turns out, does exist" [but the "proof" he cites was actually a statement taken out of context. See next paragraph.]
- P. 42. "This alone was enough for those who came with an apparent agenda to disrupt" [Eklof reaches a conclusion based on inaccurate information]

As "proof" that the disruption of the presenters' program was pre-planned, Eklof cites a LREDA Board member's October newsletter article which responded to LREDA member concerns about our choice to hire white male presenters for the LREDA conference, six months after religious educators had called for dismantling white supremacy in our UU culture. Rev. Eklof took one sentence from the newsletter article, and used it out of context. The newsletter article addressed the optics of a photograph of three white speakers (, and Odyssey speaker) in promotional material. We felt it did not represent the content or diversity of the conference. In fact, the author of the article promotes the presenters stating that " and his NVC partner, were eager to help [the LREDA Fall Conference Planning Team] develop an embodied experience in which [conference attendees] can explore the topics of power (over, between, among) and privilege (the historical systemic foundations that support racism)." https://www.lreda.org/october-2017-enews.

3.

Other inaccuracies in "The Gadfly Papers" demonstrating lack of diligence:

1. P. 40 ▬▬▬ "...segregated the whites from the persons of color. A room was then set up down the hall where the persons of color were invited to visit with the LREDA Diversity and Inclusion Team to discuss what had happened. This bias toward those representing only one identity."
    a. Using the word "segregated" is inflammatory, triggering and misrepresents the situation entirely. There was a space for people of color set up from the beginning of the conference, not after the keynote was halted. Having a separate space for people of color is an established practice at Fall Conference, General Assembly, and in many other UU spaces. This practice supports the stated needs of people of color. After the presenters were stopped, the LREDA Board set up another room for the Board and the Diversity and Inclusion Team. The people of color caucus was invited to join them; the Board and Diversity and Inclusion Team were there to listen, and determine a way forward. Again, this entire practice is common in Unitarian Universalist spaces.

2. P. 41 "...nearly two years later both men say not a single person from the UUA had ever reached out to check on them or query about the incident."
    a. The UUA was not involved in the planning or hosting of this conference. The LREDA Board did correspond with ▬▬▬ after the conference. This is another inaccurate claim.
    b. If Rev. Eklof had been diligent, he would have known LREDA is the appropriate body, and would have verified statements by the presenters by contacting LREDA leadership. If he had reached out to LREDA he would have been told, the LREDA Board did contact the presenters. One presenter and one LREDA board member exchanged brief emails a few weeks after the conference and agreed to connect later. Two LREDA board members reached out to the speakers via email in February of 2018 but the men did not respond.

3. P. 39 Rosenberg, who developed NVC based upon his personal experiences with anti-Semitism, was being characterized as a white supremacist.
    a. White supremacy is not the same as being a white supremacist

4. P. 41, "Immediately following the disastrous conference, another LREDA staff member issued a formal statement to its membership"
    a. A LREDA board member, not a staff member, wrote this formal statement. It was published as the board member's October newsletter article which was emailed to LREDA members and friends, posted on our website and shared on social media on 9-29-2017, *well before* the November conference and not immediately following the conference.

5. P.39 and 40. "Little more than an hour into the first day's program...after about 20 minutes, LREDA's President at the time, ▬▬▬ entered and reportedly said, "We're done here,"
    a. The two male presenters began on the opening night Friday, November 3rd with an evening of exercises and introduction to the program. The planned

APPENDIX C

programming was halted on the second day that the partners presented, November 4th, at roughly 10:00 am.

6. P. 39-40 "But someone in the back of the conference room became increasingly agitated by their efforts to do so and became vocally critical of NVC. "How dare you!" The person exclaimed. "I don't know what to do," ▓▓▓ finally responded, "because I keep reflecting what I'm hearing and trying to understand what's important to you, but I don't get that you trust that I hear you. Do you have that trust?" "No, I don't," the hostile attendee said. "What can I do?" ▓▓▓ asked. "Sit down and shut up!"
   a. This is hearsay since Eklof is relying on ▓▓▓ not the person "at the back of the room"

7. P. 41 "▓▓▓ verifies this same staff member had contacted him in advance of the conference expressing concern about these posts, asking, "Is there some NVC trainer who is a woman or a woman of color?" ▓▓▓ said, "yes," and offered to help contact her. His impulse in that moment told him, "This is too risky. Let's back out," but by the end of their conversation the staffer said, "No, I feel confident about it. I think you guys will be fine."
   a. **Response from LREDA Board member:** The person who spoke with ▓▓▓ was not a staff member. It was LREDA Board member, ▓▓▓ shared the concerns expressed by LREDA members about the promotional materials, which showcased all white presenters (including ▓▓▓ and ▓▓▓). She gave the presenters information about LREDA, including the White Supremacy Teach In because it was an important aspect of what was going on with LREDA at the time.
      i. ▓▓▓ did talk to ▓▓▓ about optics and asked if he knew a woman or a Person of Color presenter of Non Violent Communication. ▓▓▓ responded that "he wasn't comfortable in working with someone he didn't know". ▓▓▓ suggested several names, one of which was LREDA member, ▓▓▓, who is female and white and has had substantial anti-racism, anti-oppression, multicultural training. ▓▓▓ agreed that he would be comfortable working with ▓▓▓ asked ▓▓▓ if she could co-present with ▓▓▓ and ▓▓▓ but ▓▓▓ said she wasn't planning on attending the conference and needed time to think about it. Ultimately, she declined to be a co-presenter.

8. P. 42 "They were accused of being patronizing for coming off the speaker's platform in order to be on the same level as everyone else."
   a. LREDA provides all presenters, including ▓▓▓ and ▓▓▓ with Presenter Guidelines, that include information on accessibility. When the speakers insisted on speaking from the floor, rather than the speaker's platform despite being asked by conferees to remain there, the issue was about accessibility. Conferees told them multiple times: "We can't see you"
      i. The Presenter Guidelines state:
      "BE SEEN ......Elevate yourself if possible. And to BE HEARD Always use a microphone in non-intimate spaces." The presenters were asked to stay on the stage and not step down to the floor because people in the

5

146

back could not see them. The presenters denied several requests to step back on the stage and remained on the floor.

9. P. 43 or 44 "<u>There's nothing wrong with me.</u>' And I really recognized this was an expression of something within the UUA culture, it wasn't about me at all."
    a. Response from Rev. ▇▇▇▇▇▇▇ UUA Staff, conference attendee: "Their particular program was a mismatch for our religious educators in LREDA. It seemed to create forced intimacy, to gloss over oppression and inequality, and to engage in what many perceived as disingenuous self-centered vulnerability. Many, including me, concluded the activities and assumptions were inappropriate and even offensive. The program felt alienating and wounding to many, especially our colleagues of color.

    But Liberal Religious Educators were not going to quietly endure. We took the mic one by one and named the ways their presentation and assumptions had been hurting people of color and others ...who consistently live and work in contexts where the balance of power tilts against them. Jared showed himself not to be adequately responsive to the critique from the floor."

4.

Members of the 2017-18 LREDA Board and the 2019-20 LREDA Board are filing this complaint now due to the publication of "The Gadfly Papers" last May. The book's inaccuracies injured many people, especially those of color. We are filing this complaint on behalf of all people who were hurt by "The Gadfly Papers" in furtherance of LREDA's bylaws to support and advocate for religious educators of every age, race/ethnicity, class, gender, gender identity, physical ability and sexual orientation. Additionally, the author clearly demonstrates a lack of professional conduct as a Fellowshipped Unitarian Universalist Minister. His false and misleading description of the fall 2017 conference placed LREDA in particular, and the UUA and UUMA by extension, in a publicly degrading light.

We raise this fourth area of the Code of Conduct that Rev. Eklof has violated with his publication: "I will not engage in public words or actions that degrade the vocation of ministry or diminish among us the esteem of our calling."

Rev. Eklof's accusations that we were on a "witch hunt" against "white males" at the conference are not true. He failed to do proper diligence in reporting on the LREDA 2017 conference. The name and reputation of LREDA has been damaged in his book of one-sided assumptions.

Resolution

Members of the 2017-18 and the 2019-20 LREDA Boards ask that Rev. Todd Eklof be placed on conditional probation from membership in the MFC with the following conditions of probation:
1. Rev. Eklof will make a "Real Apology" (cited in ▇▇▇▇▇▇ podcast originally from researchers at Ohio State University); which includes:
a. An expression of regret;
b. A genuine understanding of the harm done leading to an explanation of what went wrong;
c. An acknowledgement of responsibility;
d. A declaration of repentance;

APPENDIX C

e. An offer of repair [in our case, this must include a statement of retraction];
f. A request for forgiveness.
  2. Rev. Eklof will undergo one-on-one anti-racism, anti-oppression, multicultural training by a LREDA-approved qualified consultant at Rev. Eklof's expense for two (2) years, once a month, with assigned reading.

If Rev. Eklof does not meet the conditions of probation established by the Committee, we ask that Rev. Eklof be placed on indefinite suspension or removal from Ministerial Fellowship.

In faith,

Members of the 2017-18 and the 2019-20 LREDA Boards

Members of the 2019-2020 Board

Members of the 2017-2018 Board

Impact Statements

[Ten pages of "impact statements" from eleven individuals following the formal complaint have been omitted]

THE GADFLY AFFAIR

Todd Eklof

From:	▓▓▓▓▓▓▓▓▓▓▓▓▓▓▓
Sent:	Tuesday, February 4, 2020 2:00 PM
To:	minister@uuspokane.org
Subject:	UUA Investigation

Rev. Eklof,

I have been assigned as the investigator for the complaint filed against you by LREDA. My role is to gather relevant materials, conduct interviews and write a summary with recommendations to the Office of Ethics and Safety. I see that Rev. ▓▓▓▓▓▓▓▓ has outline the general parameters of the process and has made recommendations to you regarding Policy 17 c.

To begin this process, I would like to schedule a conversation with you in the next couple of weeks to explore your reactions to complaint.
This conversation can be on zoom or we can chat on the phone. Following our conversation, it is suggested that you prepare a written response to the complaint and add any additional materials (documents. emails etc.) that support your position.

I do understand that this is a stressful and perhaps disconcerting event for your ministry. Please know that all parties will be treated fairly and with ministerial care.

I look forward to hearing from you.

Rev. ▓▓▓▓▓▓
UUA Consultant Investigator

APPENDIX C

Todd Eklof

From:
Sent: Tuesday, March 3, 2020 8:39 PM
To:
Subject: Investigation

Hi Todd,

Now that you have returned from you sabbatical, us there a convenient time for us to talk about the complaint? You can text me at ▮▮▮▮▮▮▮ .

Thanks
▮▮▮▮▮▮

THE GADFLY AFFAIR

Todd Eklof

From:	▇▇▇▇▇▇▇▇▇▇▇▇▇▇▇
Sent:	Thursday, March 5, 2020 1:03 PM
To:	Richard Davis
Cc:	Todd Eklof
Subject:	Re: from Rick Davis - Todd Eklof's Good Officer

Received, thank you.

On Thu, Mar 5, 2020, 12:55 PM Richard Davis ▇▇▇▇▇▇▇▇▇ wrote:

Dear Rev. ▇▇▇,

Rev. Eklof (Todd) and I have conferred about his response to your request for an interview pursuant to the complaint against him lodged by LREDA to the MFC. Upon reflection, he finds that he cannot in good conscience agree to participate in this inquiry. Please know that his decision is based on principle and is in no way intended as a gesture of disrespect toward you.

Regarding his decision Rev. Eklof writes: *With respect, investigating a minister for his writings is a violation of his rights as an American citizen and of his free pulpit. For the sake of our Unitarian Universalist tradition and the future freedoms of liberal ministers, I cannot in good conscience validate such proceedings with my participation. My book, our UU values, and the content of the complaint filed against me should be all that is necessary to put this matter to rest.*

Speaking as Todd's Good Officer I must concur with him that having such investigations run counter to the spirit of our free faith tradition.

Sincerely,

Rick Davis

APPENDIX C

March 6, 2020

The Rev. Todd Eklof
minister@uuspokane.org

Dear Todd –

The Rev. ▮▮▮▮▮ forwarded the following message to me (via your Good Officer, The Rev. Rick Davis):

With respect, investigating a minister for his writings is a violation of his rights as an American citizen and of his free pulpit. For the sake of our Unitarian Universalist tradition and the future freedoms of liberal ministers, I cannot in good conscience validate such proceedings with my participation. My book, our UU values, and the content of the complaint filed against me should be all that is necessary to put this matter to rest.

I'm writing in my role as the Executive Secretary of the Ministerial Fellowship Committee. I understand from your statement that you are refusing to participate in the process of investigating the misconduct charge against you. I want to be clear that refusing to participate in the initial investigation would be considered in violation of Rule 28 in the MFC Rules:

> **28. Cooperating with the Committee**
>
> It is expected that all candidates for Fellowship and all ministers in Fellowship will cooperate with the Committee at all times. This includes, but is not limited to, responses to requests for information, provision of requested documentation, attendance at meetings with the Committee, and compliance with any remediation and/or probation requirements. Non-compliance may be grounds for termination of Fellowship.

I wanted to make sure you were clear about Rule 28 when you made the statement quoted above and, if not, offer you another opportunity to participate in the investigation of the misconduct charge filed against you. With this in mind, please let me know by Thursday, March 12, 2020 if you

▮▮▮▮▮▮▮▮▮▮▮▮▮▮▮▮24 Farnsworth Street, Boston MA 02210 | P (617) 742-2100 | F (617) 367-3237

uua.org

wish to continue your refusal to cooperate with the MFC. I will inform the Committee of your decision for their consideration and action.

In peace,

The Rev.
Executive Secretary, Ministerial Fellowship Committee
Co-Director of Ministries and Faith Development

Cc: The Rev. Rick Davis, Good Officer; The Rev. ███████, Consultant for Ethics and Safety; The Rev. ███████, Chair, MFC; ███████, Executive Vice President, UUA.

APPENDIX C

The Rev. ▮▮▮▮▮▮▮
Executive Secretary, Ministerial Fellowship Committee
Co-Director of Ministries and Faith Development

March 11, 2020

Dear Rev. ▮▮▮▮▮,

Thank you for the respectful tone of your response and for the invitation to change my mind regarding my participation in your investigation: an invitation I must respectfully decline. Since writing and giving away my book of dissenting views only a few short months ago, I have been officially banned by the UUA, publicly condemned by hundreds of my colleagues, fired as an adjunct by Meadville-Lombard Theological School, censured by the UU Minister's Association, and am now being investigated by the Ministerial Fellowship Committee.

Your investigator's initial communication to me stated "all parties will be treated fairly and with ministerial care." Yet, less than 48 hours after distributing my book, this same individual signed a June 22, 2019 public letter stating "clergy of color are faced with the dissemination of racism, ableism, and the affirmation of other forms of oppression, including classism and homo- and transphobia, in a book called *The Gadfly Papers* by Todd Eklof." My book affirms nothing of the sort!!!

Given the biased and libelous public response of the investigator the MFC has chosen to oversee this matter, perhaps you will understand why I cannot reasonably trust the MFC to be a neutral party at this time. I can only interpret this investigation as being without credibility and as another example of the authoritarian turn that has become widespread within the UUA, which I most certainly do write about in *The Gadfly Papers*.

So, for now, in good conscience and for the sake of freedom of the pulpit and the freedoms of other ministers, I cannot cooperate with or legitimize this further instance of authoritarian overreach occurring within our once free and noble liberal religion.

> Therefore none of the superintendents or others shall abuse the preachers, no one shall be reviled for his religion by anyone, according to the previous statutes, and it is not permitted that anyone should threaten anyone else by imprisonment or by removal from his post for his teaching.
>
> Edict of Torda [1568]

Respectfully,

[signature: Todd F. Eklof]

Rev. Dr. Todd F. Eklof
minister@uuspokane.org

Cc: The Rev. Richard David, Good Officer

THE GADFLY AFFAIR

Todd Eklof

From:
Sent: Wednesday, March 11, 2020 6:13 PM
To: Todd Eklof
Subject: Re: From Rev. ▮▮▮ on behalf of the Ministerial Fellowship Committee

Todd

Well received.

In Peace,

▮▮▮

The Rev. ▮▮▮ | Co-Director of Ministries and Faith Development
Phone ▮▮▮ | ▮▮▮
uua.org | Twitter | Facebook

Our work is made possible by congregations' generous gifts to the Annual Program Fund and individual friends like you. Please consider making a gift today!

> On Mar 11, 2020, at 6:54 PM, Todd Eklof <minister@uuspokane.org> wrote:
>
> Dear ▮▮▮
>
> I am attaching my reply to your recent email and Rev. ▮▮▮'s letter.
>
> Thanks,
>
> Todd
>
> Rev. Dr. Todd F. Eklof
> Unitarian Universalist Church of Spokane
> 4340 W. Fort George Wright Drive
> Spokane, WA 99224

APPENDIX C

Todd Eklof

From: ▓▓▓▓▓▓▓▓▓▓▓▓▓▓▓▓▓
Sent: Monday, March 30, 2020 8:41 AM
To: minister@uuspokane.org
Cc: ▓▓▓▓▓▓▓▓▓▓▓▓▓▓▓▓▓▓▓▓▓▓▓▓▓▓▓▓▓▓▓▓▓

Subject: Update from the MFC

Dear Todd –

I'm writing to update you on the process of the complaint of ministerial misconduct filed against you by LREDA.

The Executive Committee of the Ministerial Fellowship Committee met last Tuesday and discussed the process thus far. Because you have been non-compliant with the initial investigation into this matter in violation of Rule 28 which requires cooperation with the Committee, they determined to recommend a full fellowship review to the full MFC at its business meeting on Sunday, March 29th. The motion passed, and it is now up to the Executive Committee to determine the scope of any further investigation, and to assign up to three people outside of the MFC to make up the investigating team. At this point, the Rev. ▓▓▓ will turn over her documentation to be considered by the new investigative team.

You can find the full text regarding fellowship reviews in Rule 21 of the MFC Rules, but I've edited it down to the relevant sections here:

21. Procedures for Review of Full Fellowship

If a full Committee Fellowship Review is called for, the Executive Committee will assign an investigative team from outside the Ministerial Fellowship Committee's membership, to be in contact with complainants and other individuals the team deems relevant. Information gathered by the investigative team will be shared with the Committee and with the minister.

A written notice shall be sent to the minister outlining the reasons for the Fellowship Review, all information gathered from the investigation that will be considered at the Fellowship Review, the date and location of the Fellowship Review, and the procedures which will be followed. Such notification shall be postmarked not less than one month prior to the scheduled date of the Review.

All expenses involved in the travel and appearance of the minister and the minister's Good Offices person will be borne by the Committee. All expenses involved in the travel and appearance of the complainant, or individual representatives of classes of complainants, will be borne by the Committee. The Executive Committee may invite additional representatives or complainants to meet privately with it, accompanied by an advocate designated by the Office of Ethics and Safety, if the Executive Committee deems such meeting essential to fully understand the nature of the complaint and ensure its appropriate resolution, and the Moderator of the Board of Trustees approves its payment of expenses involved in the travel and appearance of such person(s).

THE GADFLY AFFAIR

A written response to the contents of the investigation including the name of the minister's Good Offices person and any additional material the minister intends to submit for consideration is required within 14 days of receipt of the notice referred to in Rule 21C.

If a minister fails to appear at a Fellowship review, the Review will proceed in the minister's absence.

I realize that this is difficult news, and I do encourage you to seek the support and counsel of your good officer, The Rev. Rick Davis, whom I have copied. If it is your intention to decline to participate in this full fellowship review, please let me know earliest. Also, please let me know if you have any questions, which I will attempt to answer.

In peace,

▓▓▓▓▓▓▓

Executive Secretary, MFC

Cc: ▓▓▓▓▓, President UU Church of Spokane; The Rev. Rick David, Good Oficer; The Rev. ▓▓▓▓▓, Congregational Life; The Rev. ▓▓▓▓▓, Chair, MFC; ▓▓▓▓▓, Executive VP UUA; and ▓▓▓▓▓, MFC recorder.

The ▓▓▓▓▓ | Co-Director of Ministries and Faith Development, Ecclesiastical Endorser
Cell ▓▓▓▓▓ | Phone ▓▓▓▓▓ | ▓▓▓▓▓

She/Her

▲♥▲ UNIT,

Our work is made possible by congregations' generous gifts to the Annual Program Fund and individual friends like you. Please consider making a gift today!

APPENDIX C

Todd Eklof

From:	Richard Davis
Sent:	Thursday, April 23, 2020 5:28 PM
To:	
Cc:	Todd Eklof
Subject:	Re: Rev. Eklof and MFC
Attachments:	Rev Eklof and MFC.pdf

Dear Rev. ,

Please see the attached PDF for Rev. Ekof's response to your latest communication.

Todd has asked me to serve as his Good Officer in this matter and I have attached my own comments.

Sincerely,
Rick Davis

THE GADFLY AFFAIR

MFC Send

Dear Rev. ▇

Rev. Dr. Todd Eklof has asked me, serving as his Good Officer, to convey his response to your recent communication informing him that that MFC has chosen to continue its investigation against him.

First, however, I must confess to my dismay in regards to several matters.

When your email arrived *(soon after Rev. Eklof returned from a short sabbatical to tend to stress related health issues)* I opened it with the optimistic expectation that the MFC was informing Rev. Eklof that during this unprecedented time of stress and upheaval this matter would be put on hold as a compassionate, pastoral gesture. Such a pause would have allowed Rev. Eklof to attend to more urgent matters in his personal life and ministry in Spokane.

Secondly, I had further hoped that there would be some acknowledgement of the grievous misstep of appointing someone to investigate Rev. Eklof who had publicly gone on record condemning him and his book. The failure to respond to or acknowledge this lapse does not inspire trust in the impartiality of the MFC's proceedings. Nor does the fact that two members currently serving on the MFC have also publicly registered their strong condemnation of Rev. Eklof and his book.

And finally, it is perplexing and disturbing that his congregation's board president and regional UUA staff were informed of this matter before your investigation's credibility has even been determined. Who made the decision to share that information at this preliminary stage, and why did they do so? This has only served to create more chaos and confusion in the Spokane congregation.

Most Sincerely,

Rev. Rick Davis

Below is Rev. Eklof's response

> Dear Rev. ▇
>
> I object to the MFC's decision to continue with its wrongheaded and unfounded investigation of me. It is difficult to believe there is no mention of my concern regarding the very public and outlandish bias expressed by your chosen investigator, who (quite falsely) claimed I have disseminated "racism, ableism, and the affirmation of other forms of oppression, including classism and homo- and

transphobia." Unless the MFC has redefined the meaning of these offensive labels, it is unclear why I, rather than others, am being investigated for violating the UUMA code of conduct.

And relatedly, why is the MFC (a separate organization) investigating me for allegedly violating the UUMA's code of conduct? This seems to be further evidence of the conspiratorial collusion occurring between the UUA and UUMA leadership to make an example of dissenters.

The point here, however, is that your investigation, without question, has been tainted from its very inception. Yet the MFC has chosen to plow ahead without even addressing this disgrace.

I request to know the precise nature of the "ministerial misconduct" I'm being accused of?

- What authority does the MFC believe it has to pursue a complaint based on the content of a minister's published speech?
- Has the MFC conducted an unbiased preliminary examination of the legitimacy and integrity of the LREDA complaint?
- What constraints do you perceive to exist on the MFC's authority to launch such an investigation based on what is clearly a meritless complaint?
- What assurances will you make that future investigators won't have conflicts of interest, as did your first choice? Do you care?
- If it is found that the LREDA complaint is without merit (as it objectively is), what measures will the MFC take to prevent something like this from happening again, to me or any other innocent minister?
- How many MFC Board members signed any of the instant, reactive, and unfounded letters against me, which clearly do violate our ethical code of conduct?

What of the hundreds of my colleagues who have very clearly violated this code of conduct by attacking me? Do you plan investigating them with the undaunted diligence driving your investigation of me?

So, as I stated in my last communication, "for now, in good conscience and for the sake of freedom of the pulpit and the freedoms of other ministers, I cannot cooperate with or legitimize this further instance of authoritarian overreach occurring within our once free and noble liberal religion."

Todd F. Eklof

THE GADFLY AFFAIR

Todd Eklof

From: ▮▮▮▮▮
Sent: Friday, April 24, 2020 5:05 AM
To: Richard Davis
Cc: Todd Eklof
Subject: Re: Rev. Eklof and MFC

Dear Rick and Todd –

Well received. I will review your questions, confer with the MFC, and get back to you.

In peace,

Sarah

The Rev. ▮▮▮▮▮ | Co-Director of Ministries and Faith Development, Ecclesiastical Endorser
Cell ▮▮▮▮▮ | Phone ▮▮▮▮▮ | ▮▮▮▮▮

She/Her

Our work is made possible by congregations' generous gifts to the Annual Program Fund and individual friends like you. Please consider making a gift today!

From: "rdavis@▮▮▮▮▮
Date: Thursday, April 23, 2020 at 8:27 PM
To: ▮▮▮▮▮
Cc: "minister@uuspokane.org" <minister@uuspokane.org>
Subject: Re: Rev. Eklof and MFC

Dear Rev. ▮▮▮▮▮,

Please see the attached PDF for Rev. Ekof's response to your latest communication.

Todd has asked me to serve as his Good Officer in this matter and I have attached my own comments.

Sincerely,
Rick Davis

APPENDIX C

May 21, 2020

The Rev. Todd Eklof
minister@uuspokane.org

Dear Rev. Eklof –

This letter is to inform you that the Ministerial Fellowship Committee has decided to convene on June 5th to consider your removal from fellowship based your continued violation of Rule 28, which is defined as follows:

> **28. Cooperating with the Committee** - *It is expected that all candidates for Fellowship and all ministers in Fellowship will cooperate with the Committee at all times. This includes, but is not limited to, responses to requests for information, provision of requested documentation, attendance at meetings with the Committee, and compliance with any remediation and/or probation requirements. Non-compliance may be grounds for termination of Fellowship.*

On March 30, I informed you that the Committee had voted to move forward with a full fellowship review because your unwillingness to engage with the Committee's investigation constituted an initial violation of Rule 28. You were advised to reconsider. Following the receipt of your communication on April 24, in which you stated your continued intent not to cooperate with the Committee's review process, the Committee has determined it is suspending your fellowship review and instead moving directly to a decision on your fellowship status. The extension of the Committee's process into a full fellowship review would have provided you an opportunity to appropriately share any concerns with the MFC's process and to make the case that your actions were consistent with the rules of fellowship, but in choosing not to cooperate you have forfeited your opportunity to influence the Committee's further process.

24 Farnsworth Street, Boston MA 02210 | P (617) 742-2100 | F (617) 367-3237
uua.org

THE GADFLY AFFAIR

Today, a special meeting of the MFC Executive Committee met to review your continuing refusal to engage with the fellowship review process in preparation for the June 5th meeting. They noted that you have demonstrated a pattern of refusing to engage in dialogue around injury you have caused to others when informed that you are out of right relationship, of which your most recent Rule 28 violation is one example. Unfortunately, your refusal to engage has meant that conflicts which could have been addressed through mediated reparative conversation have instead been funneled through formal complaint processes, creating negative ripple effects across the broader faith community. The following examples of this refusal to engage have been noted in the Committee's process so far:

1. You refused to engage in a conversation with UUA Co-Moderator Mr. Barb Greve and other leaders representing LREDA and DRUUMM at General Assembly in Spokane when you initially distributed your book, causing controversy and pain for members of those communities.
2. The UU Ministers Association requested that you engage in a process of right relationship in the fall of 2019. Your refusal led to your formal censure.
3. You refused to engage in a conversation with the Rev. ▮▮▮▮ in her role as a Consultant for Ethics and Safety after the UUA received a formal complaint of professional misconduct from LREDA, as noted above.
4. Your subsequent refusal to engage with the Committee's full fellowship review.
5. We understand from UUA staff with the Pacific Western Region that you have refused to engage in a process with your own congregational leaders who feel you have harmed them, instead fomenting divisiveness within the congregation you are covenanted to serve.

Ministry is a relational endeavor, and it is a *sine qua non* of fellowship as a minister in the UUA that one be willing to engage with others when there is a concern expressed that one's words or actions have caused harm, particularly to those from historically marginalized communities. We as Unitarian Universalists are called to work to repair historic and ongoing injustices to Black, Indigenous and other People of Color, to transgender and nonbinary individuals, to those who are disabled, who are poor, and others who have been marginalized, and to do so both within and beyond our faith community. We understand you have sought to focus public attention on your critiques of the UUA's approach to this work of repairing injustice, but whether you agree with a particular approach to this work is not the essential issue in the Committee's process. Rather, the refusal to engage in dialogue with others and to be accountable for your actions is the substance of the

▮▮▮▮▮▮▮▮▮▮▮ 24 Farnsworth Street, Boston MA 02210 | P (617) 742-2100 | F (617) 367-3237

uua.org

APPENDIX C

Committee's review, and the base for which it will now consider removing your fellowship.

I will be in touch as soon as the Committee makes its determination.

In Peace,

The Rev. ▮▮▮▮
Executive Secretary, Ministerial Fellowship Committee
Co-Director of Ministries and Faith Development

Cc: The Rev. Richard Davis, Good Officer; , Board Chair, UU Church of Spokane; The Rev. ▮▮▮▮, Congregational Life Staff; The Rev. ▮▮▮▮, Chair, MFC; ▮▮▮▮, Executive Vice President, UUA.

UNITARIAN UNIVERSALIST ASSOCIATION

24 Farnsworth Street, Boston MA 02210 | P (617) 742-2100 | F (617) 367-3237
uua.org

THE GADFLY AFFAIR

Ministerial Fellowship Committee in regards to Rev Todd Eklof

To: *Ministerial Fellowship Committee of the Unitarian Universalist Association:*

As a preface to the following communication from Rev. Eklof let me affirm that I share his concerns in regards to the manner in which you, the MFC, have handled this matter from the very beginning. Your unresponsiveness and lack of transparency in regards to our expressed concerns about the impartiality of your proceedings continues to be troubling, to say the least. Then there are your misstatements in regards to the UUMA's censure of Rev. Eklof and internal matters in his congregation. This is very alarming and only serves to validate our mistrust in your proceedings.

Given all of this and more, I urge you to pause in this process and re-consider your next steps. Rev. Eklof would be willing to engage with you once you have satisfactorily responded to his legitimate questions and given genuine assurances that this process can truly be fair and unbiased.

Sincerely,

Rev. Rick Davis, acting as Rev. Eklof's Good Officer

Date: May 26, 2020

To the MFC:

I was surprised when you notified me on January 8th that you were investigating a complaint against me. Hoping this would get resolved, I waited until eventually, I notified your assigned investigator that I could not comply.

On March 11, 2020 I wrote you expressing my concerns about your appointment of a person as your lead investigator for my case, who is known to have publicly maligned me and misrepresented my writings, and I asked you how I could possibly receive a fair hearing?

You responded on March 30th without addressing this crucial issue, writing, instead, "because you have been non-compliant with the initial investigation into this matter in violation of Rule 28 which requires cooperation with the Committee, they determined to recommend a full fellowship review to the full MFC at its business meeting on Sunday, March 29th."

On April 24th I replied, expressing my astonishment at your determination to plow ahead while ignoring the issue I raised about your lead investigator's obvious conflict of interest, along with several other questions and concerns about your process. Later that day, I

APPENDIX C

received an email message from Rev. ▮▮▮▮▮▮▮ stating, "Well received. I will review your questions, confer with the MFC, and get back to you."

I had been eagerly awaiting your response to these concerns. So I was stunned to instead receive your May 21st letter stating you will be meeting on "June 5th to consider your removal from fellowship based on your continued violation of Rule 28," and then proceeding to erroneously claim it is I who have been unwilling to engage with you.

Such engagement must be a two-way street, not an authoritarian demand that I must unquestioningly comply with and do whatever you order me to do, no matter how unreasonable it might be.

Again, I cannot fully participate in your investigation until you have satisfactorily addressed my concerns and demonstrated that I will truly get a fair hearing.

Instead of acknowledging in the slightest of your initial missteps in launching this effort, you listed a handful of erroneous examples of my "pattern of refusal to engage." You bewilderingly state, for instance, that "The UU Ministers Association requested that you engage in a process of right relationship in the fall of 2019. Your refusal led to your formal censure."

Can you produce any evidence of this request? Because it's news to me. The (very public, widely distributed) letter of censure contains nothing in it to corroborate that claim. In fact, the letter was the first formal communication I received from the UUMA on the matter, which includes an invitation for me to "enter into a process of restoration" regarding the "harm" I have caused.

That's hardly an invitation to "engage."

I and my Good Officer have since formally written the UUMA leaders requesting they address several questions and concerns I have about this process before we can reasonably engage.

Like you, they have not been willing to do so. This one rebuttal is enough to cast doubt on your other "examples," including your blatantly false claim that I've "refused to engage" with the very investigator whose conflict of interest I've already written you twice about.

To claim I was censured because I've been refusing to engage is not just wrong, but deceitful: I was censured for writing a book of dissenting views, just as it would now appear is also the reason for your biased investigation and determination to bolt straight toward my disfellowship.

I once again invite you to honestly engage with me by reasonably addressing the concerns I've previously addressed:

- Assigning a person to conduct the investigation who has publicly and, in no uncertain terms, already concluded that I was wrong to publish my book [How can this remotely be a fair investigation?]
- Investigating a complaint that is patently specious on its face [Why did the MFC not do a preliminary evaluation of the complaint before deciding to confront me with it?]
- Investigating a complaint based on a gratuitous interpretation of covenants to which the complainant was not a party [The UUMA covenants are between ministers, not with non-ministerial groups such as LREDA. Why is an element of the UUA dealing with a complaint based on alleged UUMA covenants anyway?]
- Failing to address the problem that, even if having some validity, the complaint attacks my freedom of the pulpit [The MFC did not explain to me why it felt authorized to consider a matter which would have the effect of conflicting with this core right of ministry?]

Finally, I am deeply offended by your statement:

> We understand from UUA staff with the Pacific Western Region that you have refused to engage in a process with your own congregational leaders who feel you have harmed them, instead fomenting divisiveness within the congregation you are covenanted to serve.

It's clear that the UUA/MFC and its staff have been working behind the scenes with the leadership of a small faction in my congregation to undermine my ministry, even though that faction does not represent the sentiments of the great majority of our members. By doing so, it is the UUA staff that has inappropriately (and quite unethically) contributed to the divisiveness within my congregation. I consider this is an unacceptable intrusion in internal congregational matters, and completely outside the organizations' charters.

How can I or anyone else in good conscience "engage" in what is so obviously a one-sided and unreasonable process?

Nonetheless I once again invite you to reconsider your course by truly opening yourselves to a mutual process of genuine curiosity and honest engagement, rather than what, until now, has seemed another attempt to drive me out of the UUA for writing a book of dissenting views.

I would very much welcome that opportunity.

Sincerely,

Rev. Dr. Todd F. Eklof

APPENDIX C

June 7, 2020

The Rev. Dr. Todd Eklof
minister@uuspokane.org

Dear Todd,

The Ministerial Fellowship Committee met to review your fellowship status in light of your repeated refusal to cooperate with the misconduct review process.

You were first contacted by the Rev. ▒▒▒▒, Consultant for Ethics and Safety, on January 8th after the UUA received a complaint of misconduct from LREDA. Your Good Officer, the Rev. Rick Davis, responded in February that you were taking a medical leave from your congregation and would be unable to be interviewed until March. The Rev. ▒▒ responded that she would look forward to speaking with you in March, and we informed LREDA that there would be a delay because of an urgent medical issue. Later we learned that you traveled to Rick Davis' congregation in Salem OR to guest preach in February.

On March 5th, Rick Davis sent the following on your behalf to the Rev. ▒▒:

Dear Rev. ▒▒,

Rev. Eklof (Todd) and I have conferred about his response to your request for an interview pursuant to the complaint against him lodged by LREDA to the MFC. Upon reflection, he finds that he cannot in good conscience agree to participate in this inquiry. Please know that his decision is based on principle and is in no way intended as a gesture of disrespect toward you.

Regarding his decision Rev. Eklof writes: With respect, investigating a minister for his writings is a violation of his rights as an American citizen and of his free pulpit. For the sake of our Unitarian Universalist tradition and the future freedoms of liberal ministers, I cannot in good conscience validate such proceedings with my participation. My book, our UU values, and the content of the complaint filed against me should be all that is necessary to put this matter to rest.

Speaking as Todd's Good Officer I must concur with him that having such investigations run counter to the spirit of our free faith tradition.

UNITARIAN
UNIVERSALIST
ASSOCIATION

▒▒▒▒▒▒▒▒▒▒ ▒▒▒24 Farnsworth Street, Boston MA 02210 | P (617) 742-2100 | F (617) 367-3237
uua.org

THE GADFLY AFFAIR

The MFC reviewed your most recent letter of May 26th (received June 3rd) before they deliberated on June 5th. As they have made abundantly clear, they based their deliberations on Rule 28, and not on the substance of your writing or preaching.

The MFC has determined to remove you from fellowship with the UUA effective immediately based on your violation of Rule 28, which reads:

28. Cooperating with the Committee
It is expected that all candidates for Fellowship and all ministers in Fellowship will cooperate with the Committee at all times. This includes, but is not limited to, responses to requests for information, provision of requested documentation, attendance at meetings with the Committee, and compliance with any remediation and/or probation requirements. Non-compliance may be grounds for termination of Fellowship.

Because you have been removed from fellowship a public notice will be made according to the communication policies of the MFC. While you retain your ordination, please do not present yourself in a way that would imply fellowship with the UUA.

In peace,

The Rev.
Executive Secretary, Ministerial Fellowship Committee
Co-Director of Ministries and Faith Development

Cc: The Rev. Richard Davis, Good Officer; ███, Board Chair, UU Church of Spokane; The Rev. ███, Congregational Life Staff; The Rev. ███, Chair, MFC; ███, Executive Vice President, UUA.

24 Farnsworth Street, Boston MA 02210 | P (617) 742-2100 | F (617) 367-3237
uua.org

APPENDIX C

Todd Eklof

From: Todd Eklof <minister@uuspokane.org>
Sent: Tuesday, June 9, 2020 8:23 AM
To: Richard Davis
Subject: FW: UUMA Membership

From: ███████ ███████
Sent: Monday, June 8, 2020 1:44 PM
To: minister@uuspokane.org
Cc: ███████ execteam@uuma.org; ███████
Subject: UUMA Membership

Dear Todd,

We have received notice from the Ministerial Fellowship Committee that you are no longer in fellowship with the UUA. Per the UUMA bylaws, UUA fellowship is a pre-requisite for UUMA membership so we will be removing you as a UUMA member effective immediately. Some of the benefits of membership that you will lose include access to a uuma.org email address, the UUMA list serves (Chat & News) and our website. We will also notify your chapter leadership and the general UUMA membership that you're no longer a member of the UUMA.

If you have any questions feel free to contact me. We wish you well in the future.

With wishes for a joyous day,

███████

███████ | **Director of Operations, member Executive Team**
Pronouns: she/her/hers (learn more)
Unitarian Universalist Ministers Association

Phone ███████ | Fax: 617-848-0498 | ███████
uuma.org | connect.uuma.org | facebook.com/uuministers | @UUMinAssoc

"We Quit" Letter

To: UUMA Board of Trustees September 15, 2020
From: Disaffected Colleagues

We write to express our profound disappointment with recent developments in the UUMA and its new norms of thought, behavior, and procedure. We highlight below three of the most relevant events of the past year or so.

Public Letters of Condemnation from groups of colleagues (DRUMM, POCI Chapter, 'White Ministers') in June 2019 denouncing *The Gadfly Papers* and its author, Todd Eklof.

Of course it is okay to criticize published views – we might not be all of one mind about *The Gadfly Papers* ourselves. But these letters of condemnation are a stain upon our collegiality in several respects, the most prominent of which are:

* Making charges of racism, ableism, classism, homophobia, transphobia, vitriolic rhetoric, alt-right ideology, and white supremacy culture without citing any particulars.
* The rejection of reason and logic, calling them expressions of white supremacy.
* The fact that hundreds of colleagues signed one or more of these letters within 24 hours of the book's release – few could have read it, much less reflected upon it. Plus, the letters (and therefore the colleagues) preemptively reject the idea that it's necessary to read something before publicly condemning it and its author.
* The mob mentality which all this reflects – condemning hurriedly at the urging of others rather than forming one's own view of the matter. It seemed everybody was eager to get in a kick – a disgraceful scene.

The UUMA Board's censure of Todd Eklof

The Board's conduct in issuing censure has been disheartening and relationship-breaking...

* Violating the disciplinary process defined in our UUMA Code of Conduct – not just minor deviation, but dispensing with the most basic rudiments of fairness, like notification of the charges, presentation of evidence, and the opportunity to respond.
* Echoing the other letters of condemnation in disavowing logic, calling it a strategy of white supremacy culture.
* Citing no particulars from the book as evidence of its offense.
* Disingenuousness about the basis for censure:
  - In response to charges of censorship, claiming the censure was not about the content of the book, although the first sentence of the censure letter states it was about exactly that.
  - Claiming the censure was really about Eklof's 'refusal to engage' with his critics and the Board – implausible because that was never mentioned in the censure letter.
  - Most preposterous, claiming that the public letter of censure was not a disciplinary action, not a professional admonition, and not a formal reprimand (and therefore not subject to the procedures required in the Code).

1

APPENDIX C

It is heartbreaking to find the leaders of our professional association engaging in such astonishing deception and double-think. Under these standards of dishonesty, how is any genuine relationship possible, much less 'covenant' or 'beloved community'?

When challenged on its behavior, the Board might have said, *"Upon reflection, we were wrong to censure the way we did. We panicked under pressure. We have re-thought the matter and will [a] rescind the illegitimate censure, and [b] pursue a fresh course of action consistent with our rules and our covenantal values."* This could have included a genuine discussion of *Gadfly* and its effects (rather than a uni-directional scold), or even a fresh censure process on a legitimate basis. But in the present state of UUMA culture, that was evidently not a viable avenue for the Board. Condemnation must be swift and unquestioning, or one's status as an 'ally' of the oppressed may be in question.

June 2020 Annual Meeting

The most recent and decisive event was the approval by the UUMA membership of an overhaul of our Code of Conduct. The new approach was said to be 'more covenantal,' and yet greatly amped up rules and enforcement. Although some features of the new Code have merit, in several important respects it is deeply disturbing...

* Some of the new offenses outlined in the Code are outrageous, if not patently absurd...
  - It is now Bullying & Emotional Abuse (defined in the Appendix) to exhibit a pattern of:
    - *"challenging a person's perceptions, opinions, and thoughts."*
    - *"switching topics"* or
    - *"using words or other means to stop a conversation."*

    This is so absurd as to require no further comment.

  - The new offense of Tokenism (defined in the Appendix) includes: *"any superficial gesture"* or *"sense by a member of the dominant group of fulfilling an ethical mandate, of 'doing the right thing,' or of avoiding criticism"* in efforts toward diversity, equity, and inclusion. While superficial gestures can indeed be irksome, it is outrageous – perhaps fanatical – to mandate diversity, equity, and inclusion but then make it misconduct to seem to be doing it to fulfill a mandate.

* Language throughout the new Code conveys the implicit presumption of guilt and places the aggrieved colleague almost entirely in control of the process – an apparent rejection of the very notion of fairness.

* Perhaps most shocking is the complete elimination of due process in the enforcement of our Code. This is chilling in itself. Further, it is indicative of fanaticism that our colleagues see it as 'covenantal' to discipline or expel a member without even specifying the offending behavior and providing opportunity to respond to the allegations.

* In the amendments debate, 'con' statements seldom even addressed the merits of the amendment in question. Most implied that any criticism of the proposed overhaul, no matter how carefully measured and reasoned, was a kind of oppression, inflicting fresh trauma upon marginalized colleagues.

This whole dispiriting episode dispelled for us any remaining doubt that our professional association has become entranced with an illiberal, even anti-liberal, ideology.

2

THE GADFLY AFFAIR

Conclusion

Numerous letters have been sent by colleagues to the Board expressing alarm at the growing dogmatism and intolerance in our UUMA. A group from Return to a Democratic Faith met with Board representatives in April 2020 for a detailed discussion of the Board's conduct in issuing censure, and its implications. The discussion was civil, but produced no genuine engagement with the concerns raised. In June 2020, amendments were proposed to mitigate the worst aspects of the Code overhaul, which were not only rejected by 85-90% of the membership but unfairly characterized as hostile.

It is apparent the UUMA leadership and a large majority of members now reject the Enlightenment values which have always been baseline conditions of our faith and have inspired social progress for several centuries. These values have been replaced by a vision of cultural revolution, guided by identity politics and White Supremacy Culture jargon. Ritual confession of identity-based guilt and virtue-signaling are now primary practices. We may be supportive of many of the anti-oppressive *aspirations* of this movement, but find the dogmatism and the unreflective revolutionary fervor repugnant and destructive.

Despite (for many of us) long years of cherished ministerial collegiality, the UUMA has become for us an inhospitable place and an embarrassment. As it has been made clear that genuine dialog on the new orthodoxy will not be tolerated in our ministerial association, we cannot in good faith continue our association with it.

And so, with great sorrow, we withdraw our membership from the UUMA.

Signed,

Rev. ███████ – 28 years in UU ministry (23 parish)
Rev. Rick Davis - 35 years (all parish) - Good Officer
Rev. ███████ - 44 years (15 parish)
Rev. ███████ - 51 years (40 parish) - UUMA Exec/Board, Good Officer, Settlement Rep
Rev. ███████ - 22 years (all parish) - Chapter President
Rev. ███████ - 49 years (38 parish) - Chapter President
Rev. ███████ - 40 years (36 parish) - Chapter President, Commission on Appraisal
Rev. ███████ - 59 years (17 parish) MFC, UUA staff
Rev. ███████ - 41 years (33 parish) - Chapter President, Settlement Rep
Rev. ███████ - 61 years (35 parish)
      Social Justice Grants Panel, UUSC Assoc. Director, IARF North American Coordinator
Rev. ███████ - 18 years (all parish)
Rev. ███████ - 41 years
Rev. ███████ - 50 years (14 parish) - Chapter President, Good Officer

APPENDIX D

UUA Re-Covenanting Task Force Reports & Recommendations

- Jan. 2016 – Report of the UUA Task Force on Covenanting to the UUA Board
- Apr. 14, 2017 – Recommendations of UUA Board Task Force on Re-Imagining Covenant
- Oct. 6, 2017 – Update to Report of the Re-Imagining Covenant Task Force

THE GADFLY AFFAIR

Report of the UUA Task Force on Covenanting to the UUA Board

January 2016

Rev. ███████ Convener
███████
Rev. ███████
███████
Rev. ███████
███████
Rev. ███████

In October of last year, Moderator ███ charged the Task Force on Covenanting with imagining a future for our association in which congregations were not merely members of an organization, but related to the whole dynamically and organically: through covenants, that could be renewed periodically.

He also asked us to imagine the equivalent on the level of the local congregation, where rather than signing the relatively static membership book, people were related to the whole through a living, covenantal process.

In consultation with Moderator ███ we have seen the task force process consists of three phases: a "think tank" phase for imagining the possibilities; a phase for expanding the dialog by identifying stakeholders that need to be consulted or brought actively into the conversation; and finally a phase for developing specific recommendations to the board for bylaw and/or other institutional changes, along with pilot implementations.

We feel that we are nearing completion of the think tank part of our task.

This fascinating charge has caused us to rethink in a fundamental way what our association is, and what it might be.

According to our bylaws, Section C.2.2, "The Unitarian Universalist Association shall devote its resources to and exercise its corporate powers for religious, educational and humanitarian purposes. The **primary purpose of the Association is to serve the needs of its member congregations**, organize new congregations, extend and strengthen Unitarian Universalist institutions and, (finally), to implement its principles". The first sentence of this section provides a very general mission. The first part of the second sentence describes a membership-service organization. The UUA is, of course, comprised of its member congregations.

We should not be surprised that an association that services the very entities that comprises it would develop tendencies to be focus on internal structures, bylaws, and parliamentary method. Nor should we be surprised that in such an atomistic model reifies the independence rather than interdependence of the congregations.

Noting this quickly leads to concerns not just of efficiency, but of justice.

Successful agents in this environment are likely to be experts in certain kind of very nuanced internal and long term conversations. Activists, persons in love with movements but not membership

APPENDIX D

organizations, and all non-congregational entities are frustrated if not actively repelled. Non congregational UU identity organizations will find it easy to claim independence over accountability in times of trouble; in times of aspiration they will become confused by the extraordinary effort necessary to gain institutional toe hold at the cost of doing their work in the world.

One of the earliest conversations that we had as a task force was wondering what would happen if we just replaced covenant with membership as the means of entering into the associational box. This did not satisfy us. We notice that a lot of implementations of covenant become static because they imagine covenant as the glue between members or member equivalents; missing is the theological connection with transforming power.

But what if we thought about the purpose of the association differently?

In the past, when we have spoken of transforming governance, we have often spoken of the problem of representation, as in, congregations are not well or fully represented by delegates at General Assembly. We often invoke, even if implicitly, a model roughly equivalent to American federal democracy to understand what it is we believed we wanted from representation, and why. Congregations require representation as certain kind of singular, inviolable ontological entities; the will of these entities must have a means of articulating their concerns and interests inside of the governance structure that purports to act in their interests.

But what if congregations are not important because they are contained entities, but because they are one of many ways of manifesting and incarnating a Unitarian Universalist mission in the world? What if they don't need representation so much as they already represent various expressions of mission?

We have gestured in this direction with

"Renewing the Covenant – Ends 1.1 and 1.2 state: Congregations and communities are covenanted, accountable, healthy, and mission driven. And, Congregations and communities are better able to achieve their missions and to spread awareness of Unitarian Universalist ideals and principles through their participation in covenanted networks of Unitarian Universalist congregations and communities.

But of course, if this is what we want congregations to be, we need the associational structure to support this desire.

We've had conversations in the past about which of our governance entities is responsible for the articulation of our mission. Our bylaws give this responsibility to the board, and yet our Presidents are usually elected on platforms with visions for the association that are necessarily related to mission. Meanwhile, we also leave it to the board to article the "ends" of the association, the President to interpret them, and the staff to operationalize them.

And yet all UU organizations, congregations, regions, cooperative housing units, seminaries, identity based groups, —any gathering of two or more in the name—are already all of these things. We all own mission; we are all owned by mission; we all attempt to operationalize the mission in different ways.

What, then, if our association is actually an alliance of mission partners, all related to each other by mutual and renewing covenants: radically interdependent, mutually accountable, flexible and dynamic.

But how to initiate such a large, adaptive transformation?

One small but significant step could begin with General Assembly in 2016.

The Transforming Governance team of the board has for several years now tried to model a more engaging and generative GA process by hosting conversations where delegates have been asked large questions about their idea, preferences, and inspirations regarding our governance system. This year the team has asked our Task Force on Covenanting to perhaps help supply some content and questions to this process, with the idea that we might solicit delegate feedback precisely on this question of how a transition from membership to covenant might work.

But what if we modeled a commitment to turn away from internal questions about governance, and instead brought mission to the fore in these conversations? We could begin with asking for a response to one of our larger ends statements.

In our research as a task force, we have been much inspired by the real world example of the American Baptist Church, USA, and especially how they have restructured their general assembly equivalent, their Biennial Summit. They made a commitment to do the minimal amount of institutional business in order to devote energy instead in the "Mission Summit."

Here is how their own documents describe the Mission Summit:

The Mission Summit is the place and the time when American Baptists with diverse backgrounds, contexts and characteristics sit together, reflecting and discussing what this people of God can do in Christ's name in our world. The goal of the Mission Summit is to discern and articulate broad priorities for American Baptists for the upcoming biennium and beyond.

The Mission Summit consists of many dozens of smaller conversations, each conversation led by a trained facilitator. The conversations are grouped by three main categories—Leadership, Witness, and the Future. The conversations all begin with a question about what new shape mission requires in changing cultural circumstances. Just two examples from the 2013 conversations include:

"Can we discover new and innovative forms of church that are effective in light of today's multi-cultural and post-Christian realities?"

"Raising Up, Training, and Mobilizing Lay Leadership needs a new look. How can all God's people, each of whom has been given spiritual gifts, discover their giftedness and engage in active ministry in their communities?"

The facilitators of the conversations report on them to a group known as the Mission Table. "The Mission Table," which consists of representatives from the churches but also all mission partners (including seminaries, related organizations, etc..) is charged with collecting and refining the results of the Mission Summit, so that all mission partners can take the mission charge home to refine their own work. The Board and the Staff then, are also charged with looking to implement the mission as refined by the Mission Table.

And so, a very accessible first step would be to construct GA conversations along this model.

In terms of further steps, we might take, we can imagine at GA—but also through as many other vehicles as possible—inviting congregations and any potential mission partners-- to enter into a multi-party covenants with each other, with General Assembly, with the Board, with the President and Staff.

APPENDIX D

We can imagine this covenant would include each entity's statement of how they are living their understanding of their UU mission, and how they pledge to both support the larger movement's missional commitments, both by affirming the mission but by also participating as possible in as many opportunities for mutual clarifying and expanding the understanding mission. All parties could suggest changes to the covenant, and it would be understood that some mission partners might enter into the covenant for limited periods.

In science language, this would look like measuring the velocity (the enactment of missional work, behavior) of the particles (congregations and communities), whereas we have previously been measuring the position periodically (congregation with a mailing address and membership).

The Mission Summit might be the paradigm for these covenant creating conversations, but they could should take place everywhere-in regions, clusters, congregations, identity groups, and related organizations.

Initially these covenants could simply run alongside the existing relationships as spelled out in the bylaws, but obviously, we are also imagining a redefinition of the purpose of the association, and we can easily see recommending that eventually, the covenanting relationship replace membership.

A next step could be to look into how to develop a parallel process for congregations, whereby rather than recruit members, they invite persons to affirm and rearticulate their mission through the vehicle of covenanting and recovenantting on a regular basis.

The Task Force considers it an honor to participate in these engage and important questions; thank you for this opportunity; we are eager for continued conversation.

Recommendation of UUA Board Task Force on Re-Imagining Covenant

Summary Recommendation: The Task Force recommends that the UUA Moderator call for a General Conference of Unitarian Universalists as soon as possible and no later than the fall of 2018, for the purposes of exploring what the UUA is called to be and to do in today's world. We further recommend that the Unitarian Universalist Association schedule general conferences on a regular basis, perhaps in biennial rotation with General Assembly business sessions. Prior to merger in 1961, both the American Unitarian Association and the Universalist Church in America separated the business meetings from ecclesiastical gatherings that fostered deeper discernment of the underlying theology and philosophies of the respective movements. These conferences were unfortunately abandoned at the time of consolidation. The Task Force believes it is time to bring them back. Further, the Task Force believes that the organization DNA of the UUA be re-assessed given the racist, sexist, and class biases that formed and which are reinforced by our structure, precluding the full realization of covenantal relationships.

Definition of a "General Conference":

Both the Unitarians and the Universalists, like almost all denominations, have historically had two wings, the administrative and ecclesiastical bodies. Traditionally, administrative wings are responsible for providing services to the congregations and to the larger world on behalf of the congregations such as the congregations cannot practicably assume themselves. The ecclesiastical body is an intentional community of delegates who come together for the mutual strengthening of the congregations, the creation of relationships of mutual aid and accountability, and theological discernment. The ecclesiastical body is responsible for discerning the religious movement's ultimate and broad purpose. Ultimately, the ecclesiastical body asks and discerns answers to the question: "what is the purpose of Unitarian Universalism in these times?"

A General Conference is an ecclesiastical meeting of delegates from congregations. These general conferences should be smaller than our current General Assembly, so that meaningful discussions can be held. We might, for example, limit congregations and covenanted communities to two delegates. Every effort should be made to make these conferences affordable, so that attendees are not limited to older people of means. Further, so that these conferences can build for the future of our movement, we should actively engage youth, young adults, UUs of color, and other historically under-represented groups. The conferences should engage in one or two large questions in depth over the course of several days. It should be without activities that not directly advance the focused conversation.

Historical Background in Greater Detail:

In American Unitarianism, the ecclesiastical function was fulfilled by rather informal "Autumn Conventions" until the American Unitarian Association President Henry Bellows created the National Conference of Churches in 1865, to operate separately from the AUA itself. In 1911, the National Conference was renamed the General Conference. In 1923, the AUA, under the leadership of President Samuel Eliot, proposed subsuming the functions of the General Conference into the AUA. This was achieved in 1925, and biannual autumn meetings were established to fulfill what had been the General Conference functions (the business meetings of the AUA were held annually and separately). However,

APPENDIX D

even the committee recommending the changes warned that the functions of the General Conference would need to be maintained in the new structure so that the congregations' collective discernment of broad vision not be lost under administrative control. The editor of the Christian Register at the time wrote: "It was and is the Conference, from which the principle of creative thought and action of the free church has emanated….it has ever been the guardian of our religious liberty…the forum of unrestrained practical discussion and doctrinal disputation, and best of all, It may be, the quickening heart and will from which has largely come the missionary activity and financial resources that have builded our name…." When the Commission on Appraisal makes its "Unitarians Face a New Age "report in 1936, it is concerned that Unitarianism was losing its effectiveness and sense of mission precisely because the AUA administration had not adequately valued and attended to the functions of the conference, and that the AUA had not managed to earn high "regard and affection" enjoyed by the Conference. The Commission on Appraisal recommended that the importance of the biennial conference meetings "be enhanced in every possible way," and that a new officer, the Moderator, be established as the safeguard of this function.

The Universalists had the opposite experience of the Unitarians. Where the Unitarians were unique among American denominations in having a strong administrative body that came to dominate the ecclesiastical, the Universalists were more typical in that they first enjoyed a robust councils, conferences, and conventions, that later sought to take on bureaucratic functions. The Universalist system by the early twentieth century was comprised of vigorous state conventions, and a weak national general convention. Administrative tasks were handled almost entirely by volunteer committees, with the eventual addition of paid superintendents. A large step towards the development of an administrative body occurred in 1919, when the general superintendent as well as the heads of the Sunday school society and various auxiliary organizations too up headquartering together in Boston, and established for the first time, a Universalist mailing address. Gradually the General Superintendent came to be known as the chief administrative officer of the denomination (as opposed to the volunteer President of the General Convention), and in 1938 the General Convention took on the name of The Universalist Church of America to represent the combined ecclesiastical and administrative functions of the body.

With the consolidation of Unitarianism and Universalism in 1961, neither the functions of the Unitarian General Conference not the Universalist Convention were carried over into the Unitarian Universalist Association; historians believe that a mistake and an oversight. However, there is no provision for the ecclesiastical structure to the support the Board in that function. Ironically, the preparation for consolidation was done through the Unitarian conferences and Universalist conventions. It is quite possible that consolidation would have never been possible without these platforms for discussion and discernment. The Universalist pattern of polity, with its emphasis on the exclusively administrative role of the chief executive officer, is somewhat reflected in the UUA bylaws in the provisions that ascribe the ultimate vision power to the Board of Trustees.

We also strong urge the systemic reexamination of the roles and responsibilities enshrined in our current bylaws as we know this organization to have been derived from explicitly racist, sexist, and classist principles. The standard non-profit organization structure, first evolved in the early 19th century, was itself a copy of the business corporation, and specifically, a small New England business corporation that saw virtue in consolidating power to a limited number of patrons. The 1825 establishment of the AUA was very much a part of this milieu (see *The Transformation of Charity in Postrevolutionary New England* by Conrad Edick Wright), and while there have been many changes since that time some core patterns of distributing power remain the same. Indeed, in many ways the UUA maintains much of the structure given it by Samuel Atkins Eliot (American Unitarian Association President, 1900-1927; some even call the UUA the "House that Sam built"). Eliot did work to deliberately match the AUA organization with that of business models, especially in terms of disempowering the Board, along the lines of successful "banks, insurance companies, and mills." Of course, in doing so, he was also bringing the AUA even more in line with how wealthy New England families were accustomed to running New England charities. Eliot brought this same lens to his work as a Bureau of Indian Affairs Commissioner, where his stump speech was "From the Scalping Knife to the Can Opener," a statement about how only assimilation to white culture would save Native Americans from their own "barbarism."

Rationale for the Task Force's Recommendation:

The Task Force was charged changing the culture of the UUA from one of a member services administration to one of mutual covenanting. After over a year and a half of deep discussions, we have realized that this culture of covenant was precisely what was created by the conferences and conventions of our past, as they were designed for the mutual strengthening of the congregations, the creation of relationships of mutual aid and accountability, and theological discernment. We moreover realized that there is no reason to eliminate the administrative culture but rather supplement it. The Task Force was aided in its understanding by realizing that it was impossible to design an experience of covenant/conference within in a General Assembly. The nature of business meetings, governed by *Robert's Rules of Order*, is fundamentally adversarial rather than covenantal. Further, the General Assembly business agenda, workshop schedule, and competing distractions do not allow the time for a deep, immersed discernment on purpose and mission. And most of all the lesson of history has been that subsuming the conference structure to the administrative is in the very least ineffectual and perhaps even not possible.

Further, we cannot help but think that if we had continued holding General Conferences, we could have addressed concerns raised during the Black Empowerment Controversy in a manner that fostered deep listening and healing, and transformed individuals, our congregations, and our Association. The Business Sessions of General Assembly, on the other hand, could not help but foster either/or thinking, allowing little opportunity for creative problem-solving. Similarly, General Conferences could have addressed issues of sexism, homophobia, transphobia, ableism, and ageism in transformative ways.

More Specific and Forthcoming Recommendations:

The Task Force recommends that we take time at the 2017 General Assembly during general sessions to educate regarding our larger recommendation, but not attempt to create any experiences that would be reflective of the new culture (we now believe this is impossible). We do, however, encourage and

APPENDIX D

support the UUA Board in conducting Business Sessions of General Assembly 2017 to allow for meaningful and constructive conversation of the issues of white supremacy in UUA structures and culture. This recommendation addresses both what is and is not on the agenda, and how discussions are conducted and moderated.

We acknowledge that as a group of white UUs, members of the Task Force are not in a position to see how our recommendation may represent a white culture response to the question of re-imagining covenant. We believe it is important for us to seek feedback from BLUU, DRUUMM, UUs of Color, our GLBT communities, our communities of differing abilities, young adults, youth, and those of low income. We understand that traditional and historical practices of the Unitarians, the Universalists, or the UUA will necessarily reflect the dominant white, male, straight, middle/upper class, and ableist who created and maintained these institutions. We will begin, but not likely complete, this work by General Assembly 2017.

The Task Force will bring to the 2018 General Assembly recommended bylaw changes that would require member congregations and covenanting communities to renew their connection to the UUA biennially, with a vote of intention to join, and a statement of how they understand their community to be fulfilling Unitarian Universalist purpose.

After the initial General Conference, the Task Force plans to recommend bylaw changes to a future General Assembly that would reincorporate conference functions into the overall structure of the UUA. This would likely necessitate a reexamination and redefinition of the roles of president, moderator, and trustee. Part of ongoing General Conference provisions would be a process (we like the practices of the American Baptist Church's "Mission Table" process) whereby local congregations and identity groups could engage in conversations that would feed into the General Conference.

Respectfully Submitted,

Rev. Dr. ████████ Chair
████████
Rev. ████████
Rev. ████████

April 14, 2017

**Update to Report of the
Re-Imagining Covenant Task Force
October 6, 2017**

The Task Force presented its recommendations at General Assembly this past June. The recommendation for holding General Conferences apart from GA was particularly well received. Reaction from the audience was very positive. Task Force members also heard many positive comments in the hallways as we met GA attendees.

The Task Force's workshop was attended by about 35 people. (This, despite our having thought we canceled it). The Regional Leadership Group was quite enthusiastic, and eager to help. They recommended that regional conferences be considered as part of the General Conference structure.

Task Force member, Rev. ███████, shared the following observation, "I guess what I would like to say is that it seemed so incredibly well received in general session and at the workshop that in short, Unitarian Universalism is changing and needs to change and this would be a great way to help us. And the help that I think it pointed to is the need for us to deemphasize process and bring our mission back to the forefront of who we are. I think there was a deep desire to have a more complete and widespread understanding of covenant beyond the individualistic interpretation of the principles as determined by various UU individuals and entities. Also, there was a lot of excitement about us being able to forgo the trappings of GA, including the debates and votes on things like AIWs, in order to delve deeper into the calling of our faith and how we can find a common ground to unite us...Personally, I found Susan's report on the beginnings of the association and the links to systems of capitalism and supremacy to be a good enough reason to call us together to revisit the mission/vision and covenant of the association no matter what".

In addition to the recommendation for a General Conference to examine the theological underpinnings of our UU faith, the Task Force has also considered the use of gatherings to help set the Ends/Priorities of the UUA. The latter was addressed in our January 2017 report, recommending the UUA examine the model used by the American Baptist Church, their "Mission Table" process. We have also addressed ways in which congregations and covenanted communities enter into covenant with the UUA, and with each other. We offered the example of periodic, affirmative, renewal of covenant rather than our current system of membership.

The Task Force is aware that since we prepared our April 2017 report, there have been developments that might require a different approach to our work. Specifically, the Commission on Institutional Change will be examining all aspects of our UUA culture and structure. The Purposes and Principles section of our Bylaws will also be examined by a study commission as the result of votes at GA on the proposed "Eighth Principle". The work of the Task Force, and of these other Commissions, need to be coordinated to avoid confusion, duplication of effort or inconsistent recommendations.

The Task Force asks that the Board provide us with direction on how to proceed from here:

- Shall we continue to reach out to UU groups for feedback on the concept of a General Conference?
- Should the Task Force further develop a process for revising the UUA Ends Statement?

APPENDIX D

- Shall we recruit additional members for the Task Force, particularly UUs whose perspectives are not represented on the Task Force now? (E.g., People of Color/Indigenous, Young Adults, Persons with Disabilities)
- Shall we also elaborate, and seek feedback on, recommendations relating to bylaws changes on how congregations and covenanted communities enter into covenant with the UUA and with one another?
- How should the work of this Task Force be integrated into the work of other commissions addressing related issues?

Task Force members are willing to continue to serve. We await the Board's pleasure.

Re-Imagining Covenant Task Force
Rev. ███████ Chair
Rev. ███████
Rev. ███████

BIBLIOGRAPHY

Adams, James Luther, *On Being Human Religiously*, Stackhouse, Max L., ed., Beacon Press, Boston, MA, 1976

Bradbury, Ray, *Fahrenheit 451*, Simon and Schuster Paperbacks, New York, NY, 1951, 2013

Plato, *Apology* (pp. 11-12). Kindle Edition

Davies, A. Powell, *America's Real Religion*, Beacon Press, Boston, MA, 1947

Eklof, Todd F., *The Gadfly Papers*, Oakleaf Press, Spokane, WA, 2019

Frederick-Gray, Susan, "The Power of We," *UU World*, Spring, 2019

Freud, Sigmund, *The Future of an Illusion*, W.W. Norton & Company, New York, NY, 1961, 1989

Fromm, Erich, *Man for Himself*, Henry Holt & Company, New York, NY, 1947

Fromm, Erich, *The Art of Loving*, A Bantam Book, Harper & Row, New York, NY, 1956, 1963

Garcia-Navarro, Lulu, Interviewer, "Amélie Wen Zhao On 'Blood Heir,'" *Weekend Edition Sunday,* November 17, 2019

Grayling, A.C., *The History of Philosophy*, Penguin Press, New York, NY, 2019

Grossman, Cathy Lynn, "72% of Millennials More Religious than Spiritual," *USA Today*, April 27, 2010

BIBLIOGRAPHY

Herzog, William, R., *Jesus, Justice and the Reign of God*, Westminster John Knox Press, Louisville, KY, 2000

Howe, Charles A., *For Faith and Freedom*, Beacon Press, Boston, MA, 1997

Hughes, Coleman, "Toward a Better Anti-Racism," Manhattan Institute, www.manhattan-institute.org, August 19, 2020

Manji, Irshad, *Don't Label Me*, St. Martin's Press, New York, NY, 2019

McDowell, Esther, *Unitarians in the State of Washington*, Frank McCaffrey Publishers, 1966

McWhorter, John, "Kneeling in the Church of Social Justice," *Reason.com*, June 20, 2020

McWhorter, John, "The Virtue Signalers Won't Change the World," *Atlantic*, December 23, 2019

Murray, Pauli, *Common Ground*, "An American Credo," Winter, 1945

Munsey, Brenda, ed., *Moral Development, Moral Education, and Kohlberg*, Religious Education Press, Birmingham, AL, 1980

Pew Research Center, *"Nones" on the Rise: One-in-Five Adults Have* [sic] *No Religious Affiliation*, The Pew Forum on Religion and Public Life, Released October 9, 2012

Kant, Immanuel, *An Answer to the Question: What is Enlightenment?* Konigsberg, Prussia, September 30, 1784

Kronman, Anthony, *The Assault on American Excellence*, Free Press, New York, NY, 2019

Legutko, Ryszard. The Demon in Democracy: Totalitarian Temptations in Free Societies, Encounter Books. Kindle Edition

Lilla, Mark, *The Once and Future Liberal*, HarperCollins, New York, NY

Orwell, George, *1984*, Signet Classics, Harcourt Inc., Penguin Group (USA), 1949

Pico della Mirandola, Giovanni, *Oration on the Dignity of Man* (1496), Optimist Books by Optimist Creations, Kindle Edition, 2018

Robinson, David, *The Unitarians and the Universalists*, Greenwood Press, Westport, CT, 1985

Russell, Bertrand, *The Wisdom of the West*, Crescent Books, Inc., Rathbone Books Limited, London, 1959

Spinoza, Baruch, *Tractatus-Theologico-Politicus* (1670)

Tarnas, Richard, *The Passion of the Western Mind,* Ballentine Books, New York, NY, 1991, 1993

Ueshiba, Morehei, *The Art of Peace,* Stevens, John, Trans & Ed., Shambala Press, Boston, MA, 2002

UUA Bylaws, Section C.2.2., "Report of the UUA Task Force on Covenanting to the UUA Board," January 2016

INDEX

1

1984, 76–77

A

Academy of Motion Picture Arts and Sciences, 96
Adams, John Quincy, ii
Age of Reason, ii
allergy to authority and power, 82, 89
American Revolution, ii
Anabaptists, i
Antiquity, 1, 3
Aristotle, 2
    Aristotle's logic, 2

B

Banned, 8
Beloved Community, 83
Binding Arbitration, 52–53
Bradbury, Ray, 77–79, 97

C

Calhoun, John C., ii
Calvin, John, i, 16
Covenant, 11–14, 29–36, 65, 70, 82, 76–93
    covenantal agreement, 11
    covenantal faith, 28
    covenanting conversation, 8, 12
Critical Race Theory, vii

D

Dark Age, 95
Dark Ages, ii, 1
Dávid, Ferenc, 16
Davies, A. Powell, ii
Davis, Richard, 28–34, 37, 43, 45–52, 60, 62, 68–69, 73, 88
Democracy, ii
Diet of Torda, ii

E

Edict of Torda, ii, 62
Emersonian Transcendentalism, 81
Emperor Justinian, 2
Endarkenment, v, vii
Enlightenment, ii, 1, 24, 59, 77, 85
    Age of Reason, 4
    Enlightenment Thinking, vii
Equity, 88–89
Exceptionalism, 82, 86–89

F

Fahrenheit 451, 77–79
Fallibility, 27
Franklin, Benjamin, 5
Fromm, Erich, 78, 87

G

Gales, Joseph, ii
Giovanni Pico della Mirandola, 4
Good Officer, 28, 45, 47–52
Grayling, A.C., 1, 3

H

Healthy Congregations Team, 42, 46
Heresy, 24
Herzog, William, 95
Holy Roman Empire, 2

Howe, Charles, i
Hughes, Coleman, vi
Humanism, 3
   Religious, 5, 85
   Renaissance, 4

I

Individualism, 81–82, 86

K

Kant, Immanuel, vii, 4, 6
King John Sigismund Zápolya, ii, 16
Kronman, Anthony, 26

L

Legutko, Ryszard, 79
Lilla, Mark, 23
Logic, 25–26
Luther, Martin, i

M

Magic, 3
Manji, Irshad, vi–vii
Marduk, 79
Martin Luther King, Jr., 18, 83
McWhorter, John, vi, 17, 76
Meadville-Lombard Theological School, 5, 23, 61
Muir, Fredric, 80–93
Murray, Pauli, 18

N

Neoplatonism, 2
New York Times, 96
Nones, 86
nontheistic religion, 85

O

Original Sin, 4
Orwell, George, 76–78, 97

P

Paine, Thomas, ii
Pharisees, 95
Platonic Academy, 3
Presocratics, 2
   phusikoi, 2
Priestly, Joseph, 5
Protestant Reformation, 3

R

Red Bull, 96
Renaissance, ii, vii, 1, 3
Right Relations Team, 5, 9–10
Russell, Bertrand, 2, 3, 97

S

Safetyism, 26
Servetus, Michael, 16
Shea, Matt, iv
Sheffield Register, ii
Silver Falls State Park, 88
Socrates, 1
Spinoza, Baruch, 4
Starr King School for the Ministry, 23

T

Tarnas, Richard, 3
Task Force on Re-Covenanting, 91–93
Thales of Miletus, 2
Third Wave Anti-Racism, 17, 76
Tiamat, 79
Toulmin, Stephen, 80
Trader Joe's, 96
Trudeau, Richard, 39

U

U.S. Census Bureau, 80
Ueshiba, Morehei, 79
Unitarian Universalist Church of Salem, Oregon, vii
Unitarian Universalist Church of Spokane, 5, 54
Unitarianism
   American Unitarianism, i–iii, v, 1, 5

INDEX

UU World, 14

W

Weiss, Bari, 96
Wen Zhao, Amélie, 97

Made in the USA
Middletown, DE
23 April 2021